WORK IT!

CHRONICLE BOOKS

WORK IT!

VISUAL THERAPY's
Guide to Your
Ultimate Career
Wardrobe

by Jesse Garza and Joe Lupo

FOREWORD BY LISA AIRAN, M.D.

CHRONICLE BOOKS
SAN FRANCISCO

Library of Congress Cataloging-in-Publication Data available.

ISBN 978-0-8118-6522-7

Manufactured in China.
Designed by Omnivore.

10 9 8 7 6 5 4 3 2 1

Chronicle Books LLC
680 Second Street
San Francisco, California 94107

www.chroniclebooks.com

DEDICATION:

This book is dedicated to all women who have launched their careers or who are in the process of relaunching careers with the help of the organization Dress for Success!

We work with a lot of charities, but one of our favorites is Dress for Success. This organization is a godsend to women of little means who are entering the workforce. Read on to see how you too can make a difference. Goodness is glamorous!

Dress for Success is an international not-for-profit organization that promotes the economic independence of disadvantaged women by providing professional attire, a network of support, and the career development tools to help women thrive in work and in life. Since starting operations in 1997, Dress for Success has expanded to more than 90 cities in the United States, Canada, Jamaica, Mexico, the Netherlands, New Zealand, Poland, and the United Kingdom. To date, Dress for Success has helped more than 450,000 women work toward self-sufficiency.

You can help to give a woman a second chance by:
⇨ Volunteering at a Dress for Success location near you
⇨ Donating clothing, shoes, or accessories such as handbags and jewelry
⇨ Donating money to your local Dress for Success affiliate to support important programs and services
⇨ Conducting a suit, shoe, or accessory drive at your place of work

FOR MORE INFORMATION OR TO LOCATE A DRESS FOR SUCCESS AFFILIATE NEAR YOU, PLEASE VISIT WWW.DRESSFORSUCCESS.ORG.

TABLE OF CONTENTS

FOREWORD

Our friend and muse Dr. Lisa Airan has fused her rocket-scientist's intellect and movie-star looks to forge an unrivaled career in cosmetic dermatology. From the examination room to the red carpet, Lisa projects an image of elegance, intelligence, control, and creativity—so we thought she'd be the perfect person to inspire you by introducing this book.

Dressing for work shouldn't be a chore—getting ready to embark on your weekday can absolutely be as enjoyable as prepping for a Saturday night on the town. I am a serious doctor, but I don't take my clothing too seriously. I enjoy delighting my eye—and the eyes of those around me—with fun, fanciful fashion.

As a cosmetic dermatologist, my career and the way I present myself go hand-in-hand. I've always been attracted to beauty; I have an ability that enables me to see what's needed in order to make people look their best.

The same eye for detail that is crucial to my work reshaping people's faces is a great help in making fashion decisions, but the work I do has nothing to do with fashion per se. When I am reshaping someone's face, the decisions I make are always 100 percent individual. It's about art and architecture. Where can I add? What can I sculpt?

I feel the same way about having my own sense of style. While fashion trends change, true personal style endures, and as your confidence in making the best choices for you increases, so, I think, does your success.

Fashion is a fun hobby for me; it doesn't feel like work to express myself this way. While most doctors don't wear scrubs all day, they may feel like they have to choose more conservative pieces in order to be taken seriously. But for me, it's a personal preference to present myself the way I do. It's important to me to have fun with what I wear. I am grateful to have created a thriving practice doing what I love to do. I like to think I would be just as successful no matter what I wore—but I certainly wouldn't enjoy my career as much without the fun that fashion brings!

I've loved clothing my entire life. I was a competitive figure skater as a child and I was allowed to have complete creative direction with my skating dresses. I could choose the color and the trim; I would imagine, and then determine, exactly what the outfit was going to look like. I remember those outfits more than anything else I wore throughout my childhood because I had creative input. I'm sure that having creative freedom at a young age inspired me in terms of having a strong sense of style today.

For most of my time in medical school and in residency, I invested in a few great pieces by Jil Sander, which were architectural and refined. It didn't seem like I was going out on a limb, but I was. It was about luxury, and the super-intellectual fact that she offered everything in a million perfect Pantone shades of gray. The look was about precision and perfection—just like my own work.

Now, even though I take some serious fashion risks—my palette extends way beyond the gray scale into the entire spectrum—I won't wear things that don't look good on me just because they're fashionable. I would never force myself into a trend.

Jesse and Joe do a similar thing to what I do—they help people to look their best while remaining true to their individuality. By helping people sort through their fashion clutter—both physical and psychological—Jesse and Joe help clients and readers feel more organized and less out-of-control.

What Jesse and Joe have done for me is helped me to find the time to go through my closet. In six hours we can accomplish what would have taken me three days. Unlike so many people I've worked with, Jesse and Joe actually do everything they promise to do. The systems outlined in each of their books actually work. The more busy you are, the more you can't afford to be disorganized—I'm always wishing for ways to make my life easier, and Jesse and Joe provide them.

My style icons represent a variety of ages and sensibilities—Kate Moss, Anna Wintour, Carine Roitfeld—but what they share is an extreme confidence when it comes to their sense of style. Anything looks good if you're confident about wearing it.

That's the real reason many successful women can put almost anything together and look amazing—because their self-perception is so positive. Even in the most offbeat outfit, a successful woman walks with confidence. Her posture is good, she's got her shoulders thrown back, she strides down the street differently from the average person.

When I'm getting ready in the morning, I don't just throw on some clothes, I think, "What would I really enjoy wearing today?" Listen to your internal monitor. You know when you look really good! Everyone has days when they know they look and feel their best. That feeling should be what you're always striving for.

And with Jesse and Joe's guidance in this book, you'll always be able to achieve it.

—Lisa Airan, M.D.

INTRODUCTION

Believe it or not, we spend a third of our lives at work. Our coworkers see at least as much of us as our families do, if not more, and know us as intimately as our best friends. Still, even though we've had lots of practice getting dressed, most of us have no idea what we should be wearing to work. How can we both impress our superiors and fit in with our peers? Should one use her femininity or stifle it? What does "business casual" really mean, anyway?

As fashion stylists with our own image consulting company, Visual Therapy, we have blissfully been able to opt out of these debates. Our *job* is to dress up. And, let's face it—men have it easy. They can hardly go wrong in a suit— a centuries-old uniform. But for most women in this day and age, knowing what to wear is not so simple. That's where this book comes in.

Dressing the Part

We all know that a wardrobe can make or break a career. Would you open an account with a banker dressed in Daisy Dukes? Buy stock in a company whose CEO had food on her shirt? Hire an assistant whose bra straps were showing? Of course, skill, hard work, and aptitude are the most important things when it comes to business success, but the right outfit is often what will get you through the front door. These days, context is critically important—the jeans and boots that work in Silicon Valley just won't fly on Madison Avenue. But no matter where you work, it's in your best interest to appear current, polished, and put-together.

In our more than twenty years of image consulting, the thing that has consistently surprised us is the huge gulf between our clients' work and personal wardrobes. A woman who spends her weekends in a confident mix of cutting-edge denim, avant-garde knits, and shoes that look like art may trudge to the office in a ten-year-old suit with scuffed pumps. A woman who, in party pictures, is all aglow in a bright dress and red lipstick may appear dour in a black turtleneck and Clark Kent glasses on her company's Web site.

Glass ceilings are shattering left and right, and as women kick through the shards with their stilettos, they're finding it's no longer necessary to dress like corporate fembots or—heaven forbid—men. For better or for worse, women have more choices. We figure, as long as women are taking over the world, they might as well dress the part.

In this book, it's our aim to demystify what to wear to work. To help you determine your particular work look, we've included quizzes to tease out what your individual needs are, which colors work best for you, and which styles you'll be drawn to. It's true that every workplace has a different vibe and level of formality. To this end, we've profiled women from all sorts of industries. We worked with women from age 22 to 70, petite to plus size, in careers varying from public relations to teaching, law to engineering. These women have shared their struggles and secrets, their tips and tricks—all in the hopes of empowering women just like you.

The Way They Wore: *What's Always Worked*

Looking at women's work clothes over the past century, it's amazing that these gals got anything done. All the corsets and girdles and stockings must've made it hard to think straight! Whenever you find yourself complaining about having to wear closed-toe shoes, just remember those who came before you.

1910s

A "tailor-made"

Progressive ladies practiced their shorthand in menswear-inspired dark wool suits, called "tailor-mades." The floor-sweeping skirts and short, fitted jackets were personalized with elaborate, lacy, ruffled shirtwaists. The look may appear much more comfortable than the fussy Victorian gowns that were prevalent just a decade before, but the punishing S-shaped corset worn underneath was business as usual. Designer Paul Poiret spearheaded the movement toward a looser, more natural silhouette—perfect for lady suffragists marching for the vote.

1920s

Coco Chanel in one of her own creations

Style-setting Coco Chanel dressed Jazz Age career girls in boxy, boyish suits made of soft jersey. Hemlines rose, and flapper fashionistas made the most of their newly discovered lower legs with patterned stockings and vibrantly colored shoes.

1930s

Greta Garbo in *Sad to Be Back*

Working dames of the '30s patterned themselves after silver-screen career girls, like Greta Garbo in *Sad to Be Back* or Joan Crawford in *Mannequin*.

1940s

Joan Crawford in *Mildred Pierce*

Nobody shouldered the wartime silhouette better than Joan Crawford in movies like *Mildred Pierce*. Hollywood designer Adrian made the most of the star's linebacker proportions—and great gams—with padded wasp-waisted jackets paired with short, gored skirts. Those who couldn't get their hands on war-rationed nylons drew seams up the backs of their legs, while real-life Rosie the Riveters feminized their factory cover-ups with towering cork platforms.

1950s

A "New Look" from Dior

Dior's "New Look" brought the waist back into vogue—and the girdle along with it. Women in typing pools paired petticoat-laden skirts with sweater sets or slunk around the office in stream-lined wool sheaths. Coco Chanel made a design comeback with the instant-classic bouclé suit and a warning to retirees: "Flee boredom; it's fattening."

1960s

1960s mini-suits

Doris Day and Jackie O. set the trend with simple, elegant suits in pastel colors, worn with pointy-toed shoes and pillbox hats. The invention of panty hose allowed hemlines to rise to micromini proportions; the teensy new skirts stimulated the advent of textured tights, knee-high boots, and, in the interest of modesty, bloomerlike pantie slips. And, finally, trousers became acceptable almost any-where. (*Laugh-In* star Judy Carne made headlines when she was refused entrance at the tony 21 Club in a pantsuit; she removed her bottoms and was ushered in wearing the shortest of tunics.)

1970s

Diane von Furstenberg in her revolutionary wrap dress

The Me Decade began with Mary Tyler Moore gracing the WJM-TV newsroom in mini-, midi-, and maxi-skirts in figure-hugging polyester. Off the small screen, women were donning hot pants (with tights and platform boots) and wrap jersey dresses designed by model mogul Diane von Furstenberg. Then along came *Annie Hall*, and oversized layers made their mark in what would become known as the "soft '70s."

1980s

Melanie Griffith as Tess McGill in *Working Girl*

The hugely popular book *Women's Dress for Success* pushed ladies into masculine suits, worn with bow-neck blouses and low heels. Thankfully, innovators like Donna Karan and Liz Claiborne pio-neered mix-and-match separates for those who, like *Working Girl*'s Tess McGill, had a "head for business and a bod for sin."

1990s

A Jil Sander ad

After the excess—and shoulder pads—of the '80s, nothing seemed more modern than a streamlined pantsuit from Calvin Klein or Jil Sander, worn with a utilitarian nylon Prada bag. Casual Fridays took their place in the American workweek, bringing along with them a thousand misuses of denim and khaki.

2000s

The tailored ease of the 2000s

The first decade of the new century has been about freedom. From flannel suits to flannel shirts, women can wear what they want to the office. What's struck us most, though, is the rise of separates. Instead of buying suits, fashionistas invest in coordinating pieces they can mix and match in lots of different combinations, to show their own unique sense of style.

A SYSTEM THAT WORKS FOR YOU

Nobody loves a good system more than two obsessive organizers, so in our first two books, we explained processes for discovering your Style- and Colortypes.

Having this information on hand makes getting dressed easier and—perhaps surprisingly—more fun.

But while writing this book, we got a surprise of our own: we discovered that it's much harder to demystify the process of dressing for work than it is to help a woman discover her palette of best colors or the silhouettes and fabrics that suit her style. Discovering your Style- or Colortype is foolproof—it's as simple as looking at your skin tone, your eye color, and your favorite jacket or pair of shoes, and drawing individual conclusions. Dressing for work, however, involves all sorts of external variables: Is your industry corporate, creative, or somewhere in between? Are you a manager or a member of the support staff? Is there a formal dress code or an unspoken one? In order to progress in the company, should you make the most of your figure or hide it? The way we see it, there are three crucial things to take into consideration when putting together a work wardrobe: your Workplace, your Baseline Workstyle (what you currently wear to work), and your Worksonality (which we'll get to later).

As frustrating as it can be sometimes, your corporate culture—what we like to call your Workplace—dictates what you should wear more than any other factor. Whether a woman looks spectacular or all wrong is often a matter of context—even the most flawless evening gown appears ridiculous at Applebee's—so you must take cues on how to dress for work from the people and environment surrounding you.

Meanwhile, your work wardrobe should reflect who you really are, not hide it. That's where your Worksonality comes in. Your Worksonality describes the type of person you want to be at work. Do you want people to depend on you? You're probably a Nurturer. Do you aim to inspire? Then perhaps you're a Muse. By communicating the spirit of your professional persona through the clothing and accessories you choose, you send signals about how you want people to interact with you. And when your clothes reflect who you truly are, you'll feel confident and ready for any challenge.

The goal of all this categorization is to demystify the process of getting dressed, so you can save your blood, sweat, and tears for other things—like working.

We'll start by determining your Colortype and Styletype and then move on to determining your Baseline Workstyle and Worksonality.

DISCOVER YOUR COLORTYPE

Quiz: Which Colortype Are You?

For each question below, circle the answer that best applies to you. If you're torn between two answers, circle both of them. Our scoring process allows for multiple answers in order to give you a totally personalized palette. We've done our best to include a wide range of eye, skin, and hair colors, but everyone's coloring is unique, so choose the closest match you see here.

1   Which one of these most closely resembles your eye color?

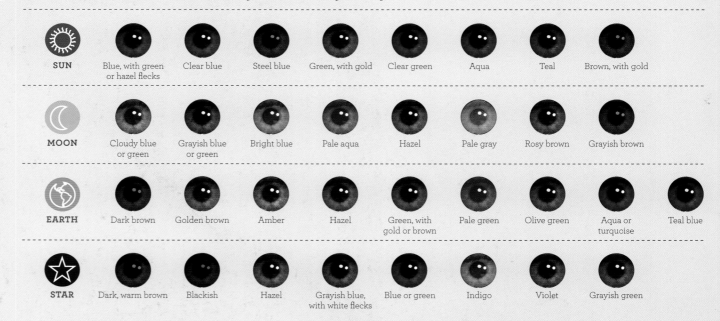

SUN — Blue, with green or hazel flecks · Clear blue · Steel blue · Green, with gold · Clear green · Aqua · Teal · Brown, with gold

MOON — Cloudy blue or green · Grayish blue or green · Bright blue · Pale aqua · Hazel · Pale gray · Rosy brown · Grayish brown

EARTH — Dark brown · Golden brown · Amber · Hazel · Green, with gold or brown · Pale green · Olive green · Aqua or turquoise · Teal blue

STAR — Dark, warm brown · Blackish · Hazel · Grayish blue, with white flecks · Blue or green · Indigo · Violet · Grayish green

2 Which one of these most closely resembles your skin color?

SUN: Your skin is warm with tawny, peachy, or golden undertones. In the sun, you tan and freckle. You blush peach. Your skin color ranges from creamy to freckly; tawny to caramel.

Famous Suns: Kristen Bell, Sarah Jessica Parker, Katie Couric, Tyra Banks.

EARTH: Your skin is warm with golden or terra-cotta undertones. You can develop a deep tan in the sun, but without sun exposure, you may be pale with little or no cheek color. Your skin color ranges from fair to bronze to brown.

Famous Earths: Teri Hatcher, Susan Sarandon, Alicia Keys, Kerry Washington.

MOON: Your skin is cool with blue or pink undertones. Moons can be ultrapale or dusky dark. If you're ultrapale you probably don't tan, but if you do, you burn first. Your skin may have a translucent quality. Your skin color ranges from ivory to rose, beige to light mocha.

Famous Moons: Sharon Stone, Marcia Cross, Cate Blanchett, Bai Ling.

STAR: Your skin is cool, or olive, with blue undertones. Stars run the spectrum from palest pale to deepest brown-black. If you are an alabaster Star you rarely tan and tend to burn, but if you are a deeper-toned Star you tan and rarely burn. Regardless, you tend not to freckle. Your skin color ranges from alabaster to pearl, deep olive to espresso.

Famous Stars: Gwen Stefani, Courteney Cox Arquette, Salma Hayek, Michelle Obama.

3 Which one of these most closely resembles the color your skin turns when you blush?

SUN: Rose, dusty coral

EARTH: Deep warm brown, overripe peach, rich pinkish coral

MOON: Bright pink, rose pink

STAR: No color, dusty rose, purplish, intense blood red

4 Which one of these most closely resembles your current hair color (natural or chemically treated)?

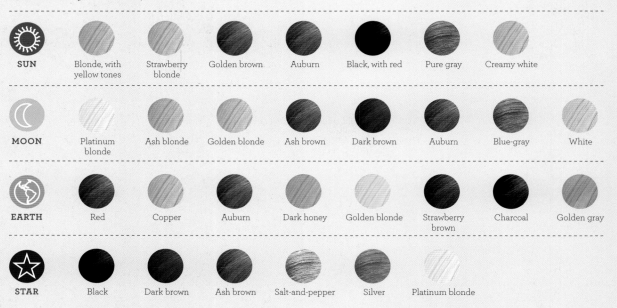

SUN | Blonde, with yellow tones | Strawberry blonde | Golden brown | Auburn | Black, with red | Pure gray | Creamy white

MOON | Platinum blonde | Ash blonde | Golden blonde | Ash brown | Dark brown | Auburn | Blue-gray | White

EARTH | Red | Copper | Auburn | Dark honey | Golden blonde | Strawberry brown | Charcoal | Golden gray

STAR | Black | Dark brown | Ash brown | Salt-and-pepper | Silver | Platinum blonde

5 Would you describe your coloring as warm or cool?

 SUN Warm   **MOON** Cool   **EARTH** Warm   **STAR** Cool

6 Which of the colors below is closest to the color of your favorite sweater or T-shirt?

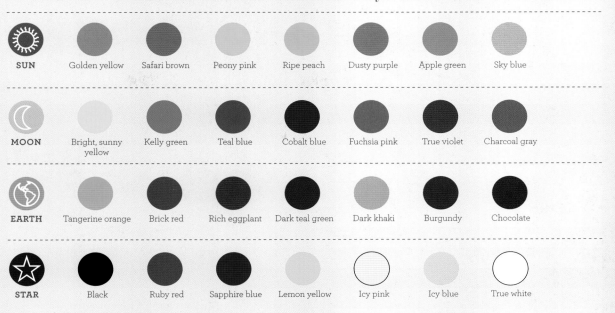

SUN — Golden yellow · Safari brown · Peony pink · Ripe peach · Dusty purple · Apple green · Sky blue

MOON — Bright, sunny yellow · Kelly green · Teal blue · Cobalt blue · Fuchsia pink · True violet · Charcoal gray

EARTH — Tangerine orange · Brick red · Rich eggplant · Dark teal green · Dark khaki · Burgundy · Chocolate

STAR — Black · Ruby red · Sapphire blue · Lemon yellow · Icy pink · Icy blue · True white

7 Which of the groups of colors below do you feel would look very unflattering on you?

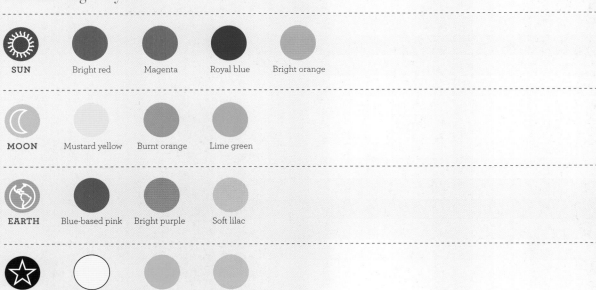

SUN — Bright red · Magenta · Royal blue · Bright orange

MOON — Mustard yellow · Burnt orange · Lime green

EARTH — Blue-based pink · Bright purple · Soft lilac

STAR — Heathered oatmeal · Warm peach · Heather green

8 If you were going to a fancy event, which of these would you wear?

SUN Beige-gold satin	**EARTH** Dark teal-green shantung
MOON Tiffany blue taffeta	**STAR** True red silk

9 Which of these colors is closest to your favorite lipstick?

SUN Sheer glossy peach	**EARTH** Deep brownish red
MOON True pink	**STAR** True blue-toned red

10 In which of these eye shadows would you not be caught dead?

SUN Blue	**EARTH** Sparkly white
MOON Deep brown	**STAR** Khaki

11 Which of these famous women share your coloring?

 SUN Mischa Barton, Jada Pinkett Smith, Gisele Bündchen, Jennifer Aniston, Vanessa Williams, Jade Jagger

 EARTH Julianne Moore, Jennifer Lopez, Julia Roberts, Oprah Winfrey, Rosario Dawson, Eva Mendes

MOON Gwyneth Paltrow, Naomi Watts, Nicole Kidman, Lucy Liu, Cameron Diaz

 STAR Jennifer Connelly, Liv Tyler, Alek Wek, Gwen Stefani, Padma Lakshmi

Now that you've completed the quiz, count the number of each icon you have circled in order to determine your primary and secondary Colortypes.

The icon you have circled most frequently is your primary Colortype. The second most frequently circled icon is your secondary Colortype.

All the colors in your primary Colortype will flatter you. Consider your primary palette to be foolproof—you should be able to hand a sales associate your palette and let him or her pick out garments in any of the colors on it.

The colors in your secondary Colortype should be selected on an individual basis and are yours to pick and choose at your own discretion. We'll explain how to know whether a color looks good next to your skin in "Testing Your Results."

Note: Unlike some older philosophies of color selection, ours deems black universally flattering. Sure, black may not be the most interesting color, but the rumors are true—it will make you look skinnier, and it provides a neutral canvas for showcasing interesting jewelry or a great pair of shoes.

Before you say, "But I look terrible in yellow!" remember that, by embarking on this process, you've agreed to approach yourself with new eyes. Don't be afraid to try all the colors on your new palette. It's possible that what looks best on you may be a major departure from what you're used to wearing. It's okay to be apprehensive, but if you jump in with both feet, you'll be amazed by the change you see in yourself, both inside and out.

Testing Your Results

Once you've found your colors, it's important to double-check that they suit you. We know what you're thinking—*If I knew which colors suited me, I wouldn't need this book!* Well, don't worry; we're going to walk you through it.

Go to the mirror. Look at the palette in your primary Colortype and find a garment in your base color. (The base color provides a foundation for each of the Colortype schemes and is clearly distinguished on the palettes.) Bunch up the fabric like an elegant scarf—yes, you could even do this with an old T-shirt—and then arrange the garment next to your face. Look at yourself, and ask these questions:

Do my eyes pop? Do they look bigger and more intense, or tired?

Does my skin glow? (It should look healthy and vibrant. The wrong color brings out flaws and signs of aging, such as broken capillaries and under-eye circles; the right color seems to make them disappear.)

Does my hair look shiny and healthy? (Even if you color it, the color should look natural alongside a flattering garment.)

Most important, how do I feel? Am I comfortable? Do I like what I see in the mirror?

If you answer "no" to any of these questions, try testing the hues in your secondary Colortype. They may actually belong in first place.

Twinkle and Jesse are both Stars

My Colortype is:

SUN

From peach to lemon, strawberry to mango, and lime to
blueberry, shades on the Sun palette are as refreshing
as summer sorbet. Suns are golden girls—so they can wear
tropical colors all year-round.

MOON

Moon women can't go wrong playing it cool – they're most gorgeous when they have the blues, from turquoise to slate, sky to Tiffany. Their cool skin tones will glow in contrast to blue-reds and pinks, from fuchsia to magenta, rose to petal.

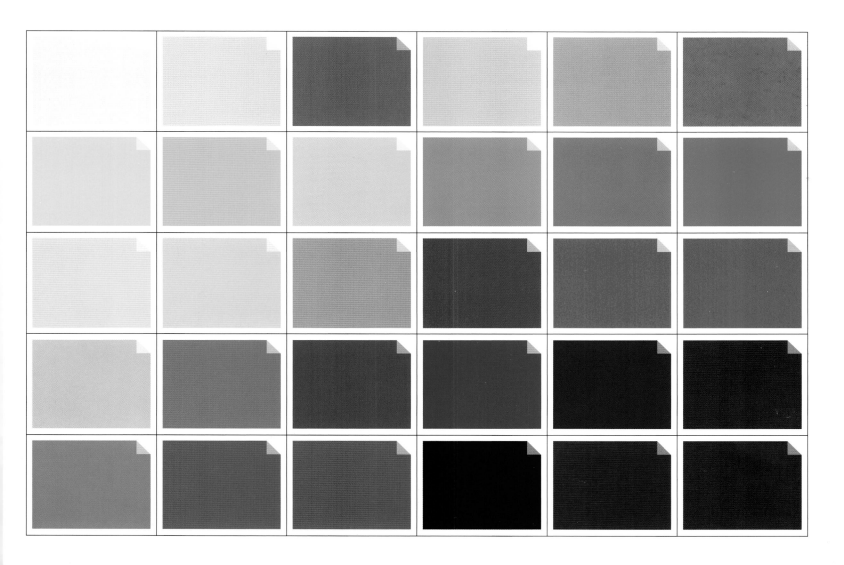

EARTH

All the sumptuous colors on the Earth palette can be found in the fairy-tale forest, from ripe shades of berry and plum to rich moss greens and browns to bright and cheery marigold, peony, and lilac.

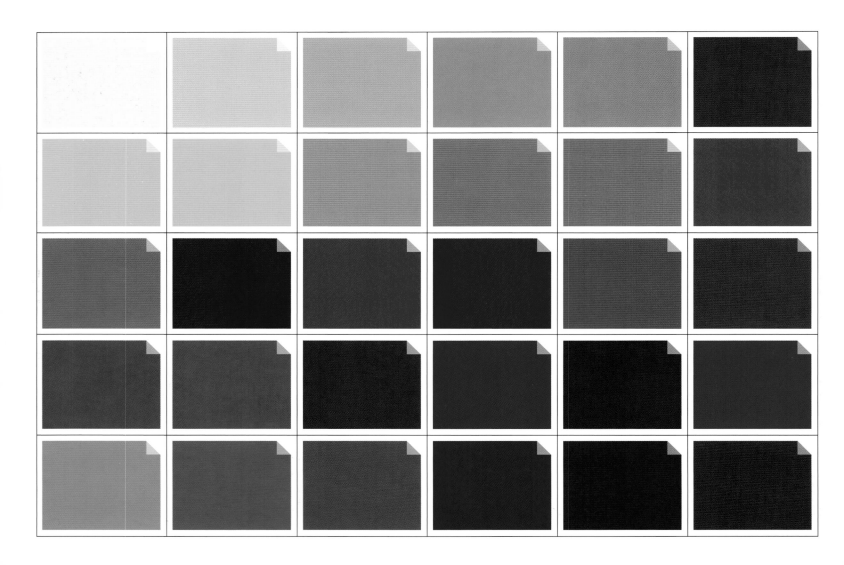

STAR

The Star comes out at night—and so do her best colors. Her palette is a wealth of modern jewel tones, from luminescent pearl to rarest emerald, ruby red to deep lapis blue.

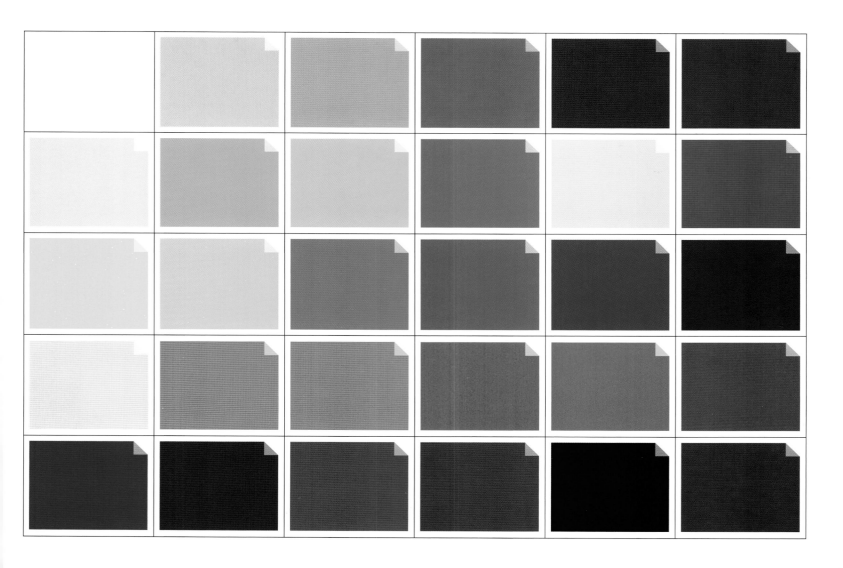

DISCOVER YOUR STYLETYPE

Quiz: What's Your Styletype?

As you take this quiz, know that there are no right or wrong answers. Circle your first impressions—what you know about your true style deep down in your gut. Don't intellectualize, or you'll just confuse yourself.

Be sure to answer every question so your scoring will be accurate.

1 If we opened your closet, which color palette would we see?

A. Black and neutrals.
B. Basics, such as navy, white, khaki, charcoal, or brown.
C. Earth tones.
D. A rainbow of colors.
E. Black with touches of bold color.

2 How would your friends describe you?

A. Playful and spirited.
B. Relaxed and liberal.
C. Sharp and direct.
D. Traditional and proper.
E. Innovative and forward-thinking.

3 Given a choice, which would you rather do?

A. Throw on a pair of jeans, a T-shirt, and funky accessories.
B. Step out in a fun floral dress or a bright mix of prints.
C. Put on a sleek V-neck top and a modern-cut pant.
D. Grab your favorite jacket, with interesting and unusual details, to wear with a black pant.
E. Get comfortable in khakis, a collared shirt, and ballet flats.

4 If someone gave you $200 for clothes, how would you spend it?

A. Buy a cashmere wrap.
B. Purchase a couple outfits at J.Crew or Banana Republic.
C. Add a slouchy suede bag to your accessories collection.
D. Buy a dress that you're sure no one else will have.
E. Splurge on anything that catches your eye.

5 When you walk into a crowded room, what would you prefer to do?

   A. Stand out.
   B. Blend in.
   C. Be in control; exude power.
   D. Seem natural and easygoing.
   E. Be zany and animated.

6 When you have the urge (or need) to go shopping, which of the following are you most likely to do?

   A. Purchase practical basics for all seasons.
   B. Head to the flea market for some great "lived-in" and funky finds.
   C. Get something with a splash of color to brighten your day.
   D. Find an unusual piece like nothing else in your wardrobe.
   E. Buy high-quality, well-tailored pieces that will always be in style.

7 When you flip through the pages of fashion magazines, what is most likely to catch your eye?

   A. The little black dresses worn by glam women in the party pictures.
   B. An editorial spread showcasing denim mixed with Moroccan textiles.
   C. A feature on a vintage fashion collection discovered in Austin, Texas.
   D. A report on new designers from Tokyo and Belgium.
   E. A Ralph Lauren lifestyle ad.

My Styletype is:

8 Which of the following best describes the decor of your home?

   A. Minimalist, architectural, and sculptural (think Jetsons).
   B. Comfortable and traditional (think Cleavers).
   C. Fun, kitschy, and unorthodox (think *Alice in Wonderland*).
   D. Lots of rugs, earth tones, and floral prints (think '70s).
   E. Streamlined, tonal, and with clean surfaces (think Tom Ford).

ANSWER KEY

How'd you do? Tally the number of times your response reflected Classic, Chic, Whimsical, Bohemian, or Avant-Garde in the space provided. The high score represents your dominant style identity, your true fashion personality; the second highest score could indicate your combination style.

1 **A.** Chic **B.** Classic **C.** Bohemian **D.** Whimsical **E.** Avant-Garde

2 **A.** Whimsical **B.** Bohemian **C.** Chic **D.** Classic **E.** Avant-Garde

3 **A.** Bohemian **B.** Whimsical **C.** Chic **D.** Avant-Garde **E.** Classic

4 **A.** Chic **B.** Classic **C.** Bohemian **D.** Avant-Garde **E.** Whimsical

5 **A.** Avant-Garde **B.** Classic **C.** Chic **D.** Bohemian **E.** Whimsical

6 **A.** Classic **B.** Bohemian **C.** Whimsical **D.** Avant-Garde **E.** Chic

7 **A.** Chic **B.** Bohemian **C.** Whimsical **D.** Avant-Garde **E.** Classic

8 **A.** Avant-Garde **B.** Classic **C.** Whimsical **D.** Bohemian **E.** Chic

Total Classic:

Total Chic:

Total Whimsical:

Total Bohemian:

Total Avant-Garde:

What Type Is Your Workplace?

As we mentioned before, the onset of Casual Fridays changed every fashion rule in the workbook. It also served to highlight the huge range of philosophies present in companies today.

In some industries, a hyper-casual environment is synonymous with innovation. For others, old-fashioned decorum and formality signal stability. Some multinational companies encourage their executives to zip around the office on Segways, while others still require employees to wear a tie every day. Where just twenty years ago every American knew exactly what to wear to the office, now she must first understand what sort of office she's reporting to.

Which brings us to the first thing you'll need to figure out about your job: its corporate culture. Which one of the following environments best describes the mood and setting of your workplace?

Casual

Technology, Media, Entertainment

➡ No one would flinch if you sat on a ball instead of a chair.

➡ It's perfectly acceptable to wear your earbuds all the time.

➡ Free candy, soda, and games are at your disposal.

➡ A colleague might express disappointment if you chose to finish a project rather than show up for your department's Wii tournament.

➡ Traditional office mores may not apply—flirting and cursing are commonplace while formality is ridiculed.

Your dilemma:
Since there are no established rules, you're writing your own. You don't want to seem square, but this is your career, and you want to be taken seriously.

You're lucky you can wear:
Casual, creative, and offbeat items.

But people might look twice—and not in a good way—if you were to put on:
A suit or anything else that would make it look like you're trying too hard.

Formal

Law, Finance, Accounting, Education

➡ Any unsolicited outburst gets a "Shhh!"

➡ Some colleagues have been around since before you were born.

➡ Company culture values respect and loyalty over innovation.

➡ You may be surrounded by dark wood and leather.

Your dilemma:
You want to fit in but prefer to look like you belong in this millennium, not the last one.

You're lucky you can wear:
Beautifully tailored suits, ladylike blouses, and heels with stockings.

But people might look twice—and not in a good way—if you were to put on:
Anything too comfortable, nontraditional, or formfitting.

Creative

→ It's not uncommon for your boss and/or assistant to comment on what you're wearing before starting a meeting.

→ E-mails about sample sales are forwarded daily.

→ Office gossip centers around haircuts and jean sizes rather than affairs and promotions.

→ When outsiders hear where you work, they may sigh and say, "I would be intimidated to work around so many beautiful women!"

Your dilemma:
You often feel as though your outside matters more than your inside, and want people to see beyond the surface.

You're lucky you can wear:
Crazy trends, adventurous hair and makeup, and nonsensible shoes.

But people might look twice—and not in a good way—if you were to put on:
Anything too relaxed or "off-trend."

Public

Medicine, Sales, Customer Service, Retail, Transportation

→ You interact more with people you don't work with than with people you do.

→ You may spend a lot of time outside.

→ You may be on your feet all day.

→ You deal with an extremely diverse group of people— you need to be a bit of a chameleon.

Your dilemma:
You feel stuck out on your own without a compass sometimes because you have little opportunity to work with colleagues. You work with more customers than colleagues, so it's difficult to determine what's appropriate for your particular work situation.

You're lucky you can wear:
Functional clothing.

But people might look twice—and not in a good way—if you were to put on:
Anything too thought-out. That might make them think you're not doing your job!

Impersonal

Manufacturing, Hospitality, Call Centers

➡ Sometimes it can seem like everyone who works with you is just passing through.

➡ While you enjoy a cordial working relationship with your boss, it's possible you've had little face-to-face contact.

➡ Sometimes you can feel more like a number than a person.

➡ Your key card is the piece of jewelry you wear most.

Your dilemma:
You feel invisible—so it's virtually impossible to care about how you look.

You're lucky you can wear:
Pretty much anything you want.

But people might look twice—and not in a good way—if you were to put on:
Anything too showy.

Home Office

Telecommuting, Home Business, Stay-at-Home Mom

➡ Technically, you don't have to get dressed, ever.

➡ You may feel like you don't have a "real" job—as though you're a fraud, pulling the wool—okay, the sweatshirt—over people's eyes.

➡ You are confronted, all day, with people trying to distract you (from children to UPS-delivery-folk, talk-show hosts to telemarketers).

➡ You often have to perform thankless tasks that interfere with your work.

➡ Your environment makes it nearly impossible for you to focus.

Your dilemma:
A person can only self-motivate so much.

You're lucky you can wear:
Your pajamas.

But people might look twice—and not in a good way—if you were to put on:
Something "fancy."

My Workplace is:

Now that you understand your Workplace a little better, turn the page to establish your Baseline Workstyle.

Discover Your Baseline Workstyle: How You're Dressing Now

Quiz: What's Your Baseline Workstyle?

Your Baseline Workstyle describes how you currently present yourself at work—not who you are inside—so don't be afraid to answer the following questions honestly. Our goal is to help you project who you truly are, and we'll use this information to help you get there.

1 **When rushing to work, you're most likely to throw on:**

   A. Loose black trousers, a T-shirt, and a cardigan.
   B. Copies of the same pieces you wore yesterday, in slightly different colors. (When you find something you like, you buy multiples.)
   C. Something you know your coworkers will comment on, whether it's a pair of vintage glasses, a funny T-shirt, or a wild print.
   D. Jeans and a T-shirt.
   E. A tight tank top, pencil skirt, and platforms.

2 **When you interviewed for your present position, you wore:**

   A. A sweater, a skirt, stockings, and sensible pumps. (You wanted to show you are serious and the job interview is about you, not your clothes.)
   B. Black trousers and a white shirt—basically, you're comfortable dressing like a waiter.
   C. A vintage dress.
   D. Your nicest jeans and a new T-shirt.
   E. A skirt with a camisole and heels.

3 **You've been given $200 to spend on work clothes. You are most likely to spend it on:**

   A. A nice leather laptop bag.
   B. A new gray pinstriped pantsuit to replace your old one.
   C. A pair of vintage glasses from the 1940s.
   D. DVDs. Who needs work clothes?
   E. Fabulous lingerie.

4 **In your current position, you wish your colleagues would:**

   A. Really listen to what you have to say.
   B. Come to you for ideas rather than advice.
   C. Appreciate your creativity but also understand that you're serious about your work.
   D. Invite you to more formal work functions.
   E. Quit looking down your dress.

5 **If you were a cinematic working girl, you'd be:**

   A. Anne Hathaway in *The Devil Wears Prada*, pre-makeover.
   B. Faye Dunaway in *Network*.
   C. Molly Ringwald in *Pretty in Pink*.
   D. Holly Hunter in *Broadcast News*.
   E. Julia Roberts in *Erin Brockovich*.

6 You would never, ever wear to work:

A. A sexy, bright red dress.
B. A totally different look from one day to the next.
C. A serious gray suit—not without a crazy neckerchief, wild shoes, and jewelry, anyway.
D. A skirt, unless you had no choice.
E. A boxy cardigan. You hate shapeless things.

7 Your hair…

A. Stays out of your way in a ponytail.
B. Has looked the same since you were 7.
C. Has been every color in the rainbow.
D. Is often wet.
E. Takes serious time and money to look its best.

8 When it's cold outside, you put on:

A. A tattered standard-issue pea coat.
B. The same style coat you've had since college, but a cashmere version.
C. A tangle of striped scarf, cardigan, and vintage puffer, all in different colors.
D. A waterproof parka.
E. A fitted, fur-trimmed jacket that barely buttons.

9 The shoes you wear most are:

A. Nondescript, black, and flat.
B. You wear all your shoes equally—you only have four pairs, and you rotate.
C. Surprisingly versatile given how crazy their color and style are.
D. Appropriate for the gym.
E. High-heeled and painful—but they make your legs look insane so they're worth it.

10 The piece of jewelry that means most to you is:

A. A small silver chain you wear under your top.
B. A tank watch that goes with everything.
C. A vintage costume piece you found on a trip abroad.
D. Jewelry?
E. A pendant that hits your décolletage at just the right point.

11 Under your desk, you keep:

A. A canvas tote for last-minute book or grocery shopping.
B. A compact umbrella.
C. An incredible piece of artwork you found on the street but haven't had a chance to take home yet.
D. A Frisbee.
E. An extra pair of peep-toe heels.

Now, tally your answers.

If you selected mostly As, you are Ms. Mousy.
You prefer to blend in rather than stand out.

If you selected mostly Bs, you are a Lady in Uniform.
You don't like surprises. Why not wear the same thing every day if it looks good?

If you selected mostly Cs, you are the Kooky Gal.
You like your clothes to be as unique as you are.

If you selected mostly Ds, you're Ms. Casual Friday.
You do your best work when you're comfortable. You have nothing to prove with your wardrobe.

If you selected mostly Es, you're a Sexy Lady.
You find power in your femininity. Why not shake what your mama gave you?

Your Baseline Workstyle tells us who you are right now but not necessarily who you want to be. Maybe you're Ms. Mousy—but only because the idea of shopping confounds you. You'd be happy to stand out a little as long as you knew you looked good and not like you were trying too hard. Perhaps you're a Sexy Lady because you know showing off your body works for you—but you secretly fancy yourself a geek.

That's where your Worksonality comes in. Turn the page to discover your Worksonality.

My Baseline Workstyle is:

Quiz: What's Your Worksonality?

Now that you understand your Baseline Workstyle a little better, it's time to discover your Worksonality. Sure, the name is a tad silly, but the idea is important: who you want to become in your working life is just as important as who people perceive you to be right now.

In order to succeed on your career path, you have to look the part—you know what they say about dressing for the job you want. Finding the right look for your personal life is all about getting your outside to match your inside, and it's the same for your career. This quiz will help you tease out your work-wear ruts, fashion crutches, and, finally, your true Worksonality.

Read through the questions below and pick the answers that best describe the person you want to be at work.

1   The feminist icon you admire most is:

   A. Eleanor Roosevelt.
   B. Hillary Clinton.
   C. Susan B. Anthony.
   D. Rosa Parks.
   E. Gloria Steinem.
   F. Jane Fonda.

2   You'd like your coworkers to see you as:

   A. Caring and supportive.
   B. Smart and decisive.
   C. Motivating and a good listener.
   D. Someone to look up to, someone who's been there.
   E. Someone who inspires creativity and helps others to see things in a new way.
   F. A trailblazer who stands on her own two feet.

3 You have a new assistant. Your first conversation together is about:

A. How she's feeling as she begins this new chapter in her life.
B. The way you would like your files organized.
C. The best ways to work together.
D. How you can help her achieve her goals.
E. The amazing Indian place you can't wait to take her to for lunch, the incredible view from the president's office, the wonderful old guy in the mailroom she has to meet.
F. That you've learned you need alone time in order to concentrate, and that this is nothing personal. You hope to help her develop the same autonomy.

4 You've just been put in charge of a group project. Before the first team meeting, you:

A. Put out the cookies you've stayed up all night baking, and prepare to assign people to roles that reflect their strengths.
B. Hand out calendars and timelines, and assign tasks and deadlines.
C. Dust off that whiteboard, and prepare for a group brainstorm.
D. Prepare to tell a story about the first team you were on and what you learned from the experience.
E. Lay out piles of old magazines, scissors, and glue sticks—you're going to make vision boards!
F. Arrange a way for everyone to check in remotely, so they can work from home.

5 Your work environment is really important to you. You always like to have:

A. A bowl of candy on your desk to entice and spoil visitors.
B. Tokens of your accomplishments—certificates, diplomas, awards—to remind you of how far you've come.
C. A comfortable, casual seating area for meetings.
D. Pictures of women you admire, inspirational quotations.
E. Photographs of trips you've taken, postcards of your favorite art, funny objects with special significance to you.
F. A clean space where you can focus without distraction.

6 You're in charge of planning a retreat for your coworkers. Which of these plans appeals to you?

A. A spa weekend with lots of communal bonding time.
B. A fitness challenge that pushes everyone's limits.
C. A few days building a home for a family in need.
D. A conference featuring successful women sharing their experiences.
E. A cultural weekend exploring museums, architecture, and foreign films.
F. An individual obstacle course with a celebratory dinner afterward, where the group will discuss personal journeys.

Turn the page for the Answer
Key and your Worksonality

And now, the Worksonalities! Please note, there's nothing literal about the Worksonality types—they are simply meant to identify character traits that will guide and inspire your work-wear choices. *Find yours below:*

If you answered mostly *A*s, you're

THE *Nurturer*

You think the way to get the best out of people is to make them feel comfortable and appreciated. You bring some of the traditional elements of being a woman into the workplace.

You'll feel like yourself in: soft lines, neutrals, interesting jewelry.

You'll feel out of place in: severe suits, head-to-toe black, pointy-toed shoes.

Nurturer Marianne Williamson

If you answered mostly *B*s, you're

THE **Director**

You pride yourself on your ability to see the big picture. You're no-nonsense and an excellent delegator. You're known as the woman with the plan.

You'll feel like yourself in: well-cut trousers, strong jackets, slim-fitting T-shirts.

You'll feel out of place in: floral dresses, flip-flops, fussy accessories.

Director Michelle Obama

If you answered mostly *C*s, you're

THE Collaborator

Your life philosophy is, Why go it alone? You know there's strength in numbers, and you get real pleasure out of group brainstorming and seeing your ideas join with another's to become something entirely new.

You'll feel like yourself in: bright cashmere knits, dark denim, comfortable boots.

You'll feel out of place in: restrictive suits, exclusive statement pieces.

Collaborator Maria Shriver

If you answered mostly *D*s, you're

THE MENTOR

You love sharing your experiences in the hopes of lighting other people's way. You've relied on insight and support from others in order to succeed, and you look forward to providing the same guidance to young people who admire you. You're a natural teacher.

You'll feel like yourself in: ladylike tops, fluid knit dresses, wedge heels.

You'll feel out of place in: anything too short or tight.

Mentor Oprah Winfrey

If you answered mostly *E*s, you're

THE

Muse

You live to make people see things in a different way—to inspire controversy and creativity. You're always in search of new experiences, and you love to expose your coworkers to new things.

You'll feel like yourself in: one-of-a-kind items found off the beaten path such as vintage pieces, statement jewelry, and dramatic color.

You'll feel out of place in: a "uniform."

Muse Sofia Coppola

If you answered mostly *F*s, you're

THE

*Indepe*ndeNT

You've never had a problem self-motivating, and you need solitude and space to develop your ideas. Rather than striving for a management role, you seek a work environment that sees your unique value and lets you do your thing without too much interference.

You'll feel like yourself in: dark knits, denim, brown leather accessories, and neutral jackets—pieces that can take you anywhere.

You'll feel out of place in: the latest trends—unless you've already been wearing them for years.

Independent Christiane Amanpour

Your Personal Profile

Now that you've taken all the quizzes, you'll have a better sense of where you are and where you want to go. List all of your results here for easy reference.

My Baseline Workstyle:

My Worksonality:

My Workplace:

My Styletype:

My Colortype:

Now, you may be shocked by the gulf between your Baseline Workstyle and your Worksonality quiz results. That's the point. Many of us get so mired in our wardrobe ruts that we forget who we really are—and, more important, who we really want to be.

Our goal is to help you adjust your Baseline Workstyle based on the results of your Worksonality quiz. We want to help you present yourself as you'd like to be seen. See the following charts for quick suggestions on how to modify your Workstyle based on your Worksonality. This will begin your style evolution.

BASELINE WORKSTYLE

Ms. Mousy

Worksonality	How to Make a Change
The Nurturer	You love to commune with others, but make sure you don't lose track of yourself. Try adding a few delicate pieces of jewelry to personalize your basic outfits.
The Director	Buy some pieces that really fit. Even if you don't feel comfortable in color (yet), you'll be amazed at how much more commanding you'll look and feel in tailored clothing.
The Collaborator	Invest in a cashmere sweater in your favorite color—especially if it's a bright one. This can serve as a conversation piece, fostering connections with colleagues.
The Mentor	Remember that you want to inspire people, and then invest in a killer jacket that will convey experience and power.
The Muse	There's a performer trapped inside you, and she's trying to get out! Go shopping, and don't come home until you buy an extremely sexy pair of shoes. You'd be amazed at how style bubbles up from the toes.
The Independent	How can you expect people to see your nonconformist spirit if you're getting lost in the crowd? Switch out your white tops for some flattering ones from your Colortype palette.

Lady in Uniform

Worksonality	How to Make a Change
The Nurturer	When you prefer to keep the focus on others rather than yourself, it might make sense to stick to a system. But why not broaden that system a bit? Add a new piece to your arsenal of basics. For example, if you always wear jackets, invest in a few cashmere cardigans to switch it up a bit.
The Director	Make sure all your go-to pieces are high quality. If you want to be in the spotlight, you have to make sure you look good close-up.
The Collaborator	It's hard to be seen as a team player if you never bring anything new to the table. Switch up your outfits a bit to convey open-mindedness, and you'll inspire others to think more creatively.
The Mentor	Dress to inspire. Always make sure that what you're wearing would impress you if you saw it on one of your employees. Consider broadening your repertoire of separates with a dress or two.
The Muse	Using your aversion to uniforms, create a collection that inspires you. Whether it's butterflies or belt buckles, creative touches are a good way to personalize your look.
The Independent	It's easy to evolve a uniform into a signature style when you're comfortable breaking away from the pack. Who says your uniform has to be solid tops and bottoms? Maybe you want to be known for luxe turtlenecks, knee-high boots, or high-design eyeglasses?

Kooky Gal

Worksonality	How to Make a Change
The Nurturer	Sometimes really loud outfits can be distancing. To communicate openness and availability, look for chunky sweaters in bright colors and fun ethnic jewelry.
The Director	Find some strong, basic pieces to anchor your funky wardrobe. You can't be taken seriously if every single thing you wear is a statement piece.
The Collaborator	Remember that when you are working in a group, the goal is to contribute, not to distract. To look more like a team player, tone down your color palette a bit—limiting yourself to one pop color per outfit is a good way to do this.
The Mentor	Make sure there's a story behind each of your special items. Pieces can inspire when they evoke memorable times from your life.
The Muse	If you are truly looking to inspire, you, and not your outfit, should take center stage. Too often, the Kooky Gal will go so wild with her ensembles that, ironically, her innovative spirit ends up getting lost.
The Independent	Look for some high-quality vintage pieces, but make sure they are classic, not costumey. When something is one-of-a-kind, it doesn't need to be loud. Even the simplest piece will stand out if no one else has it.

Ms. Casual Friday

Worksonality	How to Make a Change
The Nurturer	If your goal is to create meaningful relationships, you have to present yourself as someone people want to know—and that means no more baggy T-shirts! Try switching out your knits for a couple of woven button-downs.
The Director	Let's be honest, no one wants to take direction from someone dressed like a camp counselor. If you must wear jeans and T-shirts every day, invest in jeans cut in the most current silhouette, and make sure they fit properly; T-shirts should fit close to your body to look professional. Adding a blazer or leather jacket will convey authority.
The Collaborator	Look for cool, interesting flat shoes to wear with your casual outfits. These will serve as conversation starters (who doesn't like to talk about shoes?) and help you dip your toes into the shopping pool.
The Mentor	People are more likely to look up to you if you take pride in your appearance. Trade your jeans for some tailored trousers, and visit the cosmetics counter for some great skin care products and more polished makeup.
The Muse	Even casual clothing can be innovative. Check out athletic lines by high-fashion designers (such as Adidas by Stella McCartney) for shoes and accessories; scope out European brands (such as APC and Agnés B.) for sporty separates.
The Independent	Invest in a killer leather jacket to give all your casual outfits an edge.

44

Sexy Lady

Worksonality	How to Make a Change
The Nurturer	It's crucial that the Nurturer not dress too provocatively, or efforts to connect with coworkers could be misread. Look for high, feminine necklines and classic wide-legged trousers to mix in with your closer-fitting pieces.
The Director	Remember Demi Moore in *Disclosure*? One suit nobody looks good in is a lawsuit. If you're in charge, take the sexiness down a notch by wearing chic opaque hose with skirts and layering modest camisoles under more revealing tops.
The Collaborator	If you want colleagues to take your ideas seriously, they need to see past your figure. Try pairing some loose-fitting short dresses with opaque tights and boots for a youthful look that's not too overt.
The Mentor	You'll want to teach up-and-comers to lead with their brains, not their bustlines. To convey the strength that comes with owning your femininity, look for well-cut suits that show all the curves of the body with impeccable tailoring, not a tight fit.
The Muse	There's no question that some colleagues will be "inspired" by a woman in revealing clothing—but you want them to be getting ideas about work, not happy hour. Use color, not silhouette, to draw attention to your beauty and spirit. Nothing lights up the face like a vibrant silk top or scarf.
The Independent	There's nothing wrong with showing what you've got, especially if you don't have to answer to anyone. To ensure that you'll be properly valued by people in your professional orbit, though, make sure everything in your closet is made from high-quality fabric that doesn't pill or become transparent when stressed.

The above tips are just brief suggestions for updating your Workstyle. The transformations you'll find in the pages that follow offer concrete examples of our Workstyle process; the women featured have all learned how to express their Worksonality through their wardrobe.

You may be surprised to discover those with whom you share character traits. We hope that these quizzes will help you identify with women who seem very different from you externally, but who may have helpful style experience to share.

WORK IN PROGRESS: OUR PROCESS AND THE PROFILES

The fearless ladies appearing in this book submitted themselves to us entirely. They invited us into their homes—and their closets—and tirelessly tried on every last jacket, dress, and pair of heels they owned.

They took our Style- and Colortype quizzes and agreed to tote their best items to a photo shoot, where we would show them specific pieces chosen to round out their work wardrobes and revitalize their looks.

We asked each woman to come to our studio wearing a typical work outfit. We then spent a good deal of time talking about what she hopes to achieve in her career and what her current challenges are. When working with each woman, we took care to make choices that suited her specific lifestyle. We shopped within her budget at places she'd normally shop. We incorporated pieces from each woman's own wardrobe, whenever possible, and made an effort to use single pieces multiple ways, to minimize cost and effort. We created four different looks for each woman—looks that would take them from the boardroom to a business lunch to the company holiday party and beyond. We consulted our friend and genius beauty expert Darcy McGrath for individual hair and makeup suggestions (you'll see her insights in memos throughout the profiles).

What follows are the stories of these individual women. The stories are specific in their trials and triumphs, but universal in their appeal; we hope you'll recognize a little bit of yourself in each of them and take away inspiration, not only for your wardrobe but for your life as well.

Lindsay, 22
The Recent Grad

CAREER: Entry-level position at a textile company

BASELINE WORKSTYLE: Kooky Gal

WORKSONALITY: The Collaborator

WORKPLACE: Creative

STYLETYPE: Whimsical

COLORTYPE: Moon ☾

The Challenge:
To help Lindsay transition from girl to young woman, without leaving herself behind

The Baseline:
Lindsay came to the studio in fun, brightly colored jeans, a whimsical-print T-shirt and metallic flats, carrying a big canvas sack. She looked like the cool girl daydreaming in the back row of art history class. But the effortless, carefree attitude that can elevate someone to It-Girl status in college may be interpreted as unfocused and nonchalant in the workplace—a real handicap for Collaborators, who like to work as members of a team. This outfit will always be perfect for a Sunday brunch or flea-market date, but it needs to move from Lindsay's weekday wardrobe to her weekend one.

When you graduate from the Fashion Institute of Technology, there's no small amount of pressure to hit the ground running in the wardrobe department as you head out on your first round of interviews. But what if, even though you want to work in fashion, you're not a fashionista? "My personal style is sort of all over the place. I don't like over-the-top things; I have very few show-stoppers," Lindsay says. Growing up in a beach town, Lindsay had bummed around in shorts and bathing-suit tops in summer and sporty sweats in the winter for most of her life. Now that she's looking for a job in textile design, she's faced with the challenge of combining her casual, beachy style with the edge that being part of the fashion industry requires.

Mixing surf-shop chic and urban cool could be the recipe for a great signature style, but it also has the potential to be a recipe for disaster. Lindsay's big issue is styling—learning how to put pieces together so they make sense in different, unexpected combinations. Working at a textile company, she'll need to convey knowledge of current trends, as well as a strong sense of personal style. As a Collaborator, Lindsay wants her wardrobe to inspire communication and creativity.

Being very petite, Lindsay sometimes struggles to find clothes that she doesn't swim in (okay, corny pun; we couldn't resist). "The biggest problem is pants," Lindsay says. "Like anyone's, my weight fluctuates. I always pick up an extra five pounds in the winter." Five pounds on a 5'3" body makes a difference and means Lindsay moves between sizes 4, 5, and 6. And her height means that most jeans and pants are much longer than they need to be. "I can hem them myself—I have a sewing machine, of course! But I prefer to buy jeans that come in 'short' styles at stores like Gap and Old Navy. They're affordable and have a great fit."

As Lindsay trades in her pajama bottoms for trousers, she's starting to approach clothes in a different way. "I'm definitely becoming more conscious about how things fit and how they make my body feel overall. I am learning how to hide certain aspects and accent certain things. I try to put thought into even my super-casual outfits because, for the longest time, I didn't care what I looked like as long as I was comfortable."

Our goal was to show Lindsay that she could stay comfortable *and* look great in an industry where people automatically interpret what you're wearing as a statement about who you are.

In Bloom

Talk about an easy transition, right? Look how sophisticated jeans, a top, and a sweater look when they're worn together in a confident, polished way. The key to this outfit is fit: The jeans have a wide, extra-long leg that elongates Lindsay's lower body, and the blousiness of the floral top is reined in by a fitted, cropped sweater that hits at the tiniest, highest point of her waist. Three-quarter sleeves and a loose updo expose her long, lean arms and neck and create the illusion of even more height. "I can pair this top and sweater all the time and put whatever on the bottom," she says. And that's good thinking: when two pieces work well together, take note of the combination and treat them as a unit.

DENIM MEMO

Creating grown-up looks based around trouser-cut jeans is a painless way to start dressing more formally while staying totally comfortable. Dark denim is acceptable in most workplaces today, and high-quality weaves can look as polished as wool or flannel. Denim combines polish and approachability—two qualities crucial to being a successful Collaborator.

Blazer of Glory

Here we took the same jeans and created a 1970s, Ali MacGraw–in–*Love Story* sort of look. What girl in her early twenties doesn't look great in a romantic, but not overly feminine, ensemble? These pieces take some of the best details from menswear and translate them to a girlie silhouette. Getting Lindsay to wear this outfit took a bit of convincing: "I never would have put this one together myself. I was skeptical about the white shirt underneath, but I was pleasantly surprised! I change temperatures a lot, so I love the concept of layering."

50

STYLING MEMO

Lindsay loved the attention that the white shirt's whimsical bow brought to her face. Untied, the shirt just has two pieces of plain white fabric hanging from its neckline—the magic is all in the styling. When you buy something with a self-tie, be sure to experiment with folding and tying it lots of different ways so you can find the best one for you.

Skirting the Issue

This look is another riff on the 1970s vibe, which suits Lindsay's personality well and helps her avoid looking like she's dressed up in her mommy's clothes. Obviously, part of the outfit's youthfulness is the way it shows off Lindsay's gorgeous legs, but the unorthodox combination of accessories also projects an easygoing cool. The skinny belt brings focus to Lindsay's narrow waist, while the fuller bottom of her tunic top keeps things from getting too body conscious. Far from making her look like a lady who lunches, the floral-print silk scarf around her neck feels trendy and cool, and it lights up her face. The shrunken tweed blazer is something she'll be able to wear with everything in her closet, and the brown shoes—rather than black ones—give the look a truly original feel. "At first I didn't like the skirt, but I'm glad I decided to give it a chance—sometimes I judge too soon! And I'll admit that the brown skyscrapers were much more comfortable than I thought they were going to be."

WHEN YOU'RE WORRIED ABOUT LOOKING TOO YOUNG

Those of you who still get carded—at the movies—may struggle to be taken seriously in the workplace. Even though today youth seems to be a more-prized quality than experience, it is difficult when your ideas are dismissed based on your age.

Here are some ways to avoid being the victim of reverse ageism:

Never wear anything with a logo or a character.

Avoid typically juvenile pastel colors, such as baby pink, blue, and yellow, unless you're pairing them with neutrals.

If you're going to wear nail polish, make sure it's subtle and natural-looking.

Tame your mane: pull long hair away from your face; smooth flyaways.

Step away from the sneakers.

Make sure your lotion doesn't contain glitter.

Invest in a real coat and a few cardigans, and leave your casual jackets at home.

What a Waist

For a funkier take on the same skirt, we paired it with a fit-and-flare printed top, black tights, Mary Janes, and a contrasting turquoise beaded necklace. Our decision to pair the miniskirt with a long tunic top instead of a tucked-in blouse or short knit was unconventional but deliberate; it keeps the mini looking professional and fashion-forward rather than tarty. (No Collaborator wants to be dismissed as the sexy one.)

From the Desk of Darcy

COVERING UP: While Lindsay doesn't have any tattoos that need covering, many young people do. To hide your ink, look for a special high-coverage makeup called Dermablend, which comes in a very wide range of colors and is extra-thick and opaque. If you're wondering whether your tattoo is appropriate for work, don't be afraid to ask your boss, or someone who works in human resources.

Pleats and Thank You

If you want to highlight a girl's peaches-and-cream complexion, put her in a peach sweater. This sunny hue is like a juicy bite of summer, and, when paired with tonal shades of gray, it's sophisticated rather than bubble gum. Says Lindsay, "I was in love with that sweater! I'm not usually one for superbright, bold-color solids, but I wanted to walk home with it. It was special because it wasn't just a simple knit—the pleats gave it an unusual texture. I felt like I could pair it with a lot of stuff, from white pants to jeans to dresses."

FOOT NOTE:

When pairing shoes with a very short skirt, opt for chunky heels or flats rather than stilettos, which, in addition to looking too sexy for the workplace, throw off the silhouette, making legs look too skinny in contrast with the torso.

From the
Desk of Darcy

If everybody performed basic skin maintenance in their early twenties, they wouldn't be flocking to Botox in their late thirties. For Lindsay this means eye cream every night and high-octane sunscreen every morning.

COLOR MEMO:

To keep pastels and fruity colors from looking too young—especially important when you're a new-to-the-workplace Collaborator looking to be taken seriously—balance them with textured neutrals.

Anita, 51
The Grand Dame

CAREER: National account manager, arts and crafts company

BASELINE WORKSTYLE: Lady in Uniform

WORKSONALITY: The Director

WORKPLACE: Public

STYLETYPE: Classic

COLORTYPE: Moon ☾

The Challenge:

To convince a longtime career woman to have a teensy bit more fun with her work wardrobe—with a promise to keep her looking as competent and appropriate as ever

The Baseline:

After reading our first book, *Nothing to Wear*, Anita bought a *travel capsule*—a system consisting of a jacket, pants, skirt, and dress in the same color and fabric—to make her life easier. Great idea, but there are a couple of problems: The beige color is so close to her skin tone that it completely washes her out. And the silhouettes are a little bit dated, making her look older than someone so fit and gorgeous should. She also forgot the "pop," which would have brought some interest to a blah color palette. Since Anita is essentially a traveling salesperson, she needs to carry a lot of stuff—hence, the giant black bag. But this big black sack is too masculine and completely contradicts Anita's soft vibe and feminine features. A Director cannot afford to look weighted down by her luggage. And let's not forget the shoes—technically, an okay choice, but their toe shape and high vamps look matronly.

No one was more disappointed by the advent of Casual Fridays than Anita, who wishes she could launch a campaign to bring elegance back into the workplace. "To some extent, I'm disappointed by the way young people dress these days, and the whole idea of being an example is appealing," Anita says. "When I got out of college, it was all about that book, *Dress for Success*. If you were in the business world, you wore certain items of clothing because this was expected of you. It's amazing how some of the young women in my profession dress these days—what they think is acceptable. Cleavage is not for the workplace unless you're a cocktail waitress!"

We adore Anita's strong opinions—and her totally elegant sense of style. But we wanted to show her that conservative and appropriate don't have to mean boring. In order to make the most of her Southern belle personality, her peaches-and-cream complexion, and her Carrie Bradshaw bod, we injected a few urban pieces and strong bursts of color into her wardrobe. To really be a Director, Anita needs her wardrobe to communicate authority and know-how.

Since Anita sells products to some of the largest mass retailers in the United States, she spends a good deal of time traveling to corporate headquarters all over the country. While her office dress code is business casual, it's important that she step it up a bit when making sales calls. Even when clients themselves are dressed casually, Anita wants them to see that she has made an effort—it's good for business.

Anita is but a wisp, so we paid special attention to selecting clothing properly proportioned to her small frame. "Being petite and thin makes it hard to find things that fit properly," she says. "When you're petite, you have to wear clothing in the right scale—you don't want to be overwhelmed. Sometimes, I'll see a woman my size with a handbag so giant, she looks like a little kid carrying her mom's purse—what does that do for your credibility?"

Power Suit

Here's a much more modern capsule that serves the same purpose as her off-white number—but what a difference! It's sometimes true that dark colors can be aging. But for a true blonde Moon, like Anita, dark colors can really show off the luminescence in the skin. Instead of opting for a jacket with two buttons, we chose a single-button version to elongate Anita's torso. And we replaced her nondescript tote with a grown-up, quilted Prada bag, which serves the same purpose but has a much more flattering and current shape. We picked a bag that will travel excellently: it is featherweight; it holds a ton; and it won't lose its shape, even when folded up and stuffed into a suitcase. This is Anita's new power suit, whether she's meeting with executives at Target or inspiring her own team.

From the
Desk of Darcy

Notice how much more elegant Anita looks with soft, side-swept bangs than with her hair partially pulled back from her face. As much as it may tempt, save the partial updo for high school cheerleaders—a good blow-dry is worth every penny.

In the Jeans

The same suit jacket takes on a completely different look when worn with dark-wash jeans and a soft travel bag— perfect for a casual dinner or a flight. In fact, if Anita wears the jacket on the plane instead of packing it in her suitcase, it will be less likely to wrinkle. The dark jacket flatters her skin tone. And these suede booties look more modern than those pumps from the first photograph—we're injecting a little bit of Chic into her Classic Styletype.

56

THREE WAYS TO POP

Sometimes our clients get confused about how to incorporate their pop color into multiple pieces. No, we don't want you to buy thirty turquoise handbags. What we do suggest, though, is that you look for your pop color expressed at different levels, in different items.

Witness the magic below:

Here it is expressed in a necklace, across a variety of shades.

Here's Anita's pop color in its purest form—a bright, solid cotton T-shirt.

And here it is in the tiniest dose, as an accent color in that gorgeous paisley wrap.

58

A Crush on Ecru

Now, this is white magic! Notice how different Anita looks when her off-white dress is accompanied by a pop of color. The spectacular patterned wrap, which incorporates many of the colors from Anita's Moon palette, complements her eyes and eliminates any greige-beige washout worries. The chocolate suede kitten heels are low enough to be totally functional, but they look richer and more sophisticated than mid-heel pumps. The simple, classic silhouette of this dress evokes the timeless style of another elegant waif—Audrey Hepburn.

TRAVEL MEMO

Instead of wearing a thin scarf, bundle up in a wide, lightweight pashmina, like the one Anita's wearing here. It looks elegant when worn with a jacket or a winter coat, and on a plane, pashmina = instant blankie.

WARDROBE WISDOM

No stockings: shocking? "Recently, I read something in a magazine," Anita says, "talking about how panty hose are not as popular as they once were. Now, I know a judge who says not to show up in her courtroom without panty hose—she'll refuse to hear your case!" Many women of a certain age are horrified that stockings have mysteriously and suddenly disappeared—like bees!—but we say, embrace change. You're not going to court in this outfit. And rumor has it that Anna Wintour, legendary editor of *Vogue*, doesn't permit nylons in her office. We won't go that far. Sometimes, a pair of sleek, nude stockings is perfectly appropriate; just don't cling to them like a security blanket, especially when you have legs as good as Anita's. If you're hankering for hosiery, try opaque tights or textured hosiery.

Major Magenta

Anita is a woman who loves to dance, and this dress shows it—even when she's standing still. Normally, she would lean toward pastels, but dressing her in this deep, rich magenta number really makes the most of the natural blush of her lips and her bright blue eyes. Gold heels are the best neutral for evening; they are light and almost invisible, elongating the calves. "I would not have picked this color," Anita says. "I've never bought anything in this color! But to my surprise, it really did look good. And I love how it drapes."

FIGURE MEMO

The genius side ruching on this dress works for all body types—it can create curves on a Skinny Minnie like Anita or slim a more voluptuous body type. This is because the fabric is manipulated to create width at the shoulder and to cinch at the waist.

Anita's advice to women in their early twenties? "You never get a second chance to make a first impression, so always remember to cross your t's and dot your i's. Think about how you present yourself, and put a smile on your face. If you are paying attention, covering all the details, and pleasant to deal with, you'll do great. There are so many people who don't pay attention. People become loyal to you when you make their lives easier."

From the
Desk of Darcy

Since Anita is a true pale blonde, the more neutral her clothing, the brighter her makeup must be. I'm not talking about anything shocking—she's a Moon and has serious luminescence, so all she has to do is warm things up a little to avoid looking like Casper the Friendly Ghost. I used a rosy cream blush to bring a flush to her cheeks; she has dry skin that absorbs makeup easily, so she can carry the blush in her bag for touch-ups.

Twinkle, 35
The Firecracker

CAREER: Director of development, Uncommon Schools

BASELINE WORKSTYLE: Ms. Mousy

WORKSONALITY: The Muse

WORKPLACE: Public

STYLETYPE: Whimsical

COLORTYPE: Star ☆

The Baseline:
Twinkle came to us in this gray suit, which is a good basic look for her job. Working in nonprofit management and fundraising means moving frequently from one world to another—from her upscale office to the less affluent neighborhoods where the schools are located. Twinkle has to be equally comfortable at a donor dinner and a school lunch.

Like many working women, Twinkle relies on a couple of basic suits. But this gray wool number is so classic, it verges on blah; its perfect fit is its best asset. "My mom was a seamstress," Twinkle says. "So it's important to me to have everything truly fit my body." Twinkle likes the jacket's high stance (i.e., the distance between the neckline and the first button). The stance works well with casual underpinnings, but a lower stance would be more flattering considering her full bustline.

Our first thought upon meeting Twinkle was, "This woman has the right name." Twinkle is the kind of gal whose immediate warmth makes you feel as though you've known her forever. She devotes her life to children: her own, Morgan, four, and Jordan, ten months, and all those attending the innovative charter schools for which she fund-raises.

After five years in the high-powered world of banking, Twinkle shifted her focus from helping high-net-worth individuals invest their money to helping them donate it. She had no problem walking away from the lucrative world of private banking and into the sometimes-grueling land of nonprofits: "I had two kids in the midst of my career shift. As a mom, you really start thinking about education. It shifts your perspective." Even becoming a mom couldn't stifle Twinkle's true nature as a Muse, so we aimed to help her communicate inspiration and creativity through her wardrobe.

The circumstances under which Twinkle came to us were bittersweet. After years of taking care of her mom, who was diagnosed with stage-four breast cancer during Twinkle's first pregnancy, she decided she wanted to take care of herself. Endless flights to a faraway hospital, always with a baby in tow, had taken a toll on her, and her once-strong sense of style had quietly slipped away. Like many working moms under serious stress, Twinkle developed an intense relationship with two of the scariest words in the English language: *sweat suit*.

"I hadn't even realized the extent of my addiction," Twinkle told us. "But one year, at both Christmastime and my birthday, I got a sweat suit from every single person in my family."

We wanted to help Twinkle, well, *twinkle* again. "When my mom was sick, I wore whatever I had just to get through the day. She had always been used to seeing what she called 'Sparkle Twinkle,' but being a constant caregiver, I really let myself go. When my mom passed, I said, 'I just want to do something that she'd love to see.' So I called Visual Therapy in celebration of my mother."

Purple Reign

The first thing we wanted to show Twinkle was our *cake and frosting* concept: when you have a few excellent staples in your wardrobe (the *cake*; in Twinkle's case, two high-quality suits), you can give them a huge number of different looks with help from a few special pieces, or *frosting*. Here, Twinkle traded her suit jacket for a vibrant purple wrap dress. This style is versatile because it can be worn on its own or over pants, as Twinkle is wearing it here, bringing a sense of fun and femininity to a conservative piece. A Muse doesn't settle for a khaki trench coat—she goes for bright purple! "It's a color I would never have chosen for myself," Twinkle says, "but it just popped!"

FIGURE MEMO:

Big-busted women, take note: wrap dresses can be a bit low-cut in the front, but this doesn't mean you can't buy them. In order to avoid making Twinkle feel uncomfortable and overexposed, we layered a camisole underneath the dress.

VISITING SCHOOL SITES

WORK-TO-EVENT

Quick-Change Artist

For nights when Twinkle goes straight from work to a fund-raising event or a date with her husband, she can just slip off the pants she's wearing underneath the wrap dress, switch her big work bag for a clutch, and she's ready to go.

Berry Sleek

When we showed this piece to her, Twinkle thought she couldn't wear such a body-conscious silhouette—but just because a woman is voluptuous doesn't mean she shouldn't show her body off. Flattery is all about proportion, and this dress's wide straps, deep neckline, and narrow pencil skirt make the most of Twinkle's 1950s-film-star bod. "Despite its close fit," Twinkle says, "this dress actually made me look slimmer than I am."

The Belt Way

Just as you can deconstruct suits to create different looks for day and night, you can build in layers on top of dresses to take something formal to a more casual place. The sleek fuchsia dress from the previous look is almost unrecognizable when paired with a cozy textured jacket, tights, and boots. "I think this jacket is flattering because of its deep neckline," Twinkle says. "And, of course, I always love a big belt to draw attention to my waist. I felt like I was on the runway—this was very fun and fashionable for me. It might be a little much to take someone to school, but it's perfect for a benefit."

FIGURE MEMO:

Twinkle's jacket benefits from a cinch because she has a true hourglass shape. If your proportions are straight from chest to hip, you're better off skipping the belt and rocking some sexy heels or an open neckline. Always highlight areas you want to show off, and keep trouble spots simple so the eye glides right over them.

64

Sublime Separates

See how different the brocade jacket looks when paired with slim trousers and worn without a belt? This combination of separates is just as functional as a suit but lets Twinkle's personality shine through, even without accessories. The key to making separates—tops and bottoms that don't match but rather coordinate—look put-together is staying monochromatic. And remember that old warning against wearing blue with black? Forget it. Few color combinations are chicer. Although this look is simple, it has a real richness.

From the
Desk of Darcy

To brighten a mocha complexion like Twinkle's, try using a golden bronzer as a highlighter. Brush it on the high planes of the face—the cheekbones, brow bones, and the bridge of the nose—to show off elegant bone structure.

Asset Management

Sometimes it's hard to know what will make the most of your figure and what will overexpose it.

Here's a handy cheat sheet:

Most Prominent Element	Hides It	Maximizes It	Overexposes It
Bust	Jacket with a strategically placed button at the narrowest part of the body, just below the bustline	Deep V neckline	Strapless anything
Bottom	Wide-legged trousers	Pencil skirt	Low-rise skinny jeans
Skinny Legs	Straight-leg pants	Mini skirt	Leggings
Curvy Legs	Boot-cut jeans	A-line skirt	Pencil skirt
Strong Arms	Three-quarter sleeves	Cap sleeves	Spaghetti straps
Soft Arms	Baby-doll dress	Wrap top	Wide belt

Remember that fit is as important as style. You must avoid pieces that are too small—or too big—in order to look pulled-together. A good tailor can be your secret weapon—altering a garment to fit your body can make you look as though you've lost ten pounds.

It's too *small* if:
➡ You can't button it (this includes jackets)
➡ Fabric puckers along the seams
➡ You can't move comfortably (you should be able to sit down in pants and dresses, and to raise your hands above your head in shirts and jackets)
➡ Your bottom or bustline is constricted and loses its shape

It's too *big* if:
➡ You can grab a handful of fabric at the back of your waist
➡ Shoulder lines extend beyond your own natural shoulders
➡ The neckline exposes the tiny bow on your bra
➡ The straps keep falling down

When in doubt, buy something a size too big and have it altered to fit. It's much easier to take something in than to let it out.

STYLE COUNSEL

Advice Straight from the Hip: Jane Buckingham

Jane Buckingham is founder and president of the Intelligence Group, the trend-forecasting subsidiary of Creative Artists Agency.

When you interview a woman for a position, are there signs of grooming and dressing that you look for?

Yes, I look for someone who is well kept and who cares about the way she dresses. While I don't care at all about expensive clothes, I do care whether someone has taken the time to have a neat and well-dressed appearance. If they don't care enough to look good in an interview when they are meeting someone for the first time, then it makes me think that they may not really care about the position they are interviewing for. Also, if I am hiring for a position that involves trends, it is certainly a plus to have someone with a sense of style. And while anyone can buy style at a high price tag, it's definitely harder to pull off a cool look at a low budget, so I always admire when people are able to show their personal style without having spent a bundle.

Are there any red flags—wardrobe-wise—that make you worry about hiring someone?

Absolutely. If someone is dressed inappropriately, I get nervous. My job is about reading people, and if you don't know enough to read the interview, you won't be able to read the situations you'll get put into on the job. Red flags include clothes that are too sexy (too low-cut, too high-cut), nails that are too long or painted too bright, any offensive slogans on a T-shirt. Basically, if there is anything that a client might take offense to, I will think twice about hiring that person. I'm all for people expressing their personal style, but the fact is that this is work, and even in a company that depends on trends, we need to be respectful.

On the other hand, if someone is too stiff in her clothing or too formal, it might also be a red flag for us. Ours is a more informal work environment, and we need people who can flow with it. That would never keep us from hiring someone (after all, I think it's better to be more formal than less), but I would definitely try to make sure that the person was less stiff than her clothing choice.

How important is it to dress for work? Is it better to be overdressed or underdressed?

These days, I think it is better to be overdressed than underdressed. No one gets yelled at for being too dressed up. But being underdressed can send the wrong message—that you don't care, that you are lazy, that you don't want to be at your job. There are obviously shades of gray in how you can dress, but as the job market gets tighter, I think it will be important not only to do the best job you can while at work, but to look your best while doing it as well.

Do you notice any similarities among women—in terms of how they present themselves—who rise up the company ladder quickly?

I think women who rise quickly tend to have a style of their own. They don't copy someone else. But I also think you wouldn't define them by their clothes. They probably aren't huge fashion-risk-takers. They want to be noticed for their work, not their wardrobe. So they always look good and don't make fashion blunders, but they certainly aren't spending extra time with the stylist looking for the latest and greatest every season.

Have you ever had a wardrobe crisis during your career—maybe a size change or a need to shift your image? How did you deal with it and resolve it?

Twice. When I was seven months pregnant and covering fashion shows for television, I wanted to shoot myself. I wasn't the cutest pregnant lady, and they didn't have the cutest fashions. I decided to worry more about what I was saying than what I was wearing but also to wear clingy clothes rather than big, bulky ones. I noticed that the more I tried to hide my belly, the worse I looked; the more I showed my growing body, the better I looked (and felt!).

The second time, I felt that I didn't have enough "corporate clothes" to present to the CEOs and heads of companies with whom I was meeting. So I bought a few suits and fancy skirts and started wearing them to my power meetings. Well, I'm a trend forecaster, and not only did I feel inauthentic (and uncomfortable) in these clothes, but it turned out that the CEOs suddenly didn't find me as credible. Once I looked like them, I wasn't an authority on trends! Now I wear whatever I think speaks to the trends or looks good on me, and I don't worry about corporate politics.

In terms of presenting yourself, are there things you know now that you wish you knew at the beginning of your career?

Don't try to look richer than you are. People can spot a fake a million miles away. Better to have one real designer piece (if that matters to you) than a bunch of fakes.

What is the best way for a woman to assert her femininity without seeming overtly sexy?

Kindness. Women are typically kinder than men. We can be soft and gentle in the way we act and dress. Once we start making it too sexual or hard, it gets uncomfortable for everyone.

What are your top five dressing and grooming pet peeves for the office?

1. Long, red, acrylic fingernails (How does anyone get work done wearing those?)
2. Anything that shows too much cleavage (I don't want to show you mine; please don't show me yours.)
3. Panty hose with sandals (Sorry, I just don't like it.)
4. Supershort skirts (Save them for the evening, please.)
5. Too much perfume (It gives me migraines.)

What is your go-to work outfit—the one that makes you feel like you're going to knock everyone's socks off?

Any dress with high boots . . . something that makes me feel more comfortable than four-inch Jimmy Choo's.

Annique, 32
The Teacher

CAREER: Educator

BASELINE WORKSTYLE: Lady in Uniform

WORKSONALITY: The Muse

STYLETYPE: Chic

COLORTYPE: Moon ☾

Annique moved to the United States from Canada in 2001, and she's been on a voyage of fashion self-discovery ever since. "In Canada, everybody wears the same thing—a conservative uniform. People are not encouraged to express their individuality. Here, the expectation is to look unique. Of course it's fun to dress up, but it was difficult to make the transition!" Annique gave herself a style overhaul soon after moving to the States, when a colleague told her a crush wouldn't be interested unless she "stopped dressing so mousy." She found our first book, *Nothing to Wear,* and became a model pupil. She invested in chic separates that fit her properly—as well as more than a few pairs of femme fatale heels—and instantly fit into her sophisticated new landscape. "I used to feel like, 'I am a deep person; I don't care about superficial things.' But changing my appearance just a little has made me able to share myself with the world," Annique says. "Going through the Visual Therapy process has changed my entire life."

Now she wants to take things a step farther. While Annique's job as a teacher doesn't require her to dress up, she's considering moving into the nonprofit world and wants to start looking the part. This means adding a few serious pieces to her wardrobe in order to command authority and fit in with potential colleagues and donors, while keeping the fun pieces that make her a Muse. In addition to building her confidence for a potential career change, Annique finds that punching up her style has an unexpected effect on her students. "When you dress well, the children want to be like you. They listen to everything you say, and everything takes on a whole new meaning. Boys develop crushes, girls want to emulate you—I feel so much more effective when I pay attention to how I look."

Annique is working on her second master's degree in order to pursue a career in refugee camp education, an interest that developed when she visited Kenya to educate other teachers on how to teach reading and writing with few resources. She won't likely need too many pairs of stilettos once she embarks upon her next professional journey, but in order to get there, she has lots of networking to do; that's where these wardrobe ideas fit in.

The Future Is Bright

Just as easy and comfortable as Annique's walk-in outfit, this three-piece look works harder for her in a variety of ways. The short-sleeved jacked is an incredibly versatile piece that unites most any top and bottom and leaves its wearer feeling sophisticated. The rich indigo hue of the knit turtleneck brings attention to Annique's bright eyes and rosy complexion, and the black of the trousers makes them feel dressy. She can change her look entirely, depending on what she wears with them. "This is something I'd wear for a business meeting when I need to be taken seriously," Annique says. "I need a more serious look to build a non-profit." The rich purple hue of the turtleneck reminds Annique that, even when dressed seriously, she's still a Muse.

SHOPPING MEMO:

Jacket-of-all-trades

Many women avoid short-sleeved jackets because they think they can only be worn with short-sleeved tops, and in warmer seasons. In fact, we feel just the opposite: nothing's cuter than a colorful sleeve peeking out on a crisp fall day. Short-sleeved jackets are also more comfortable to wear indoors, especially if your office is heated.

Here's the jacket we styled four different ways. It's versatile because of its simplicity, neutral color, and interesting fabric weave. Because it has no visible buttons and a straight, rather than notched, neckline, this style looks great with a belt. And its short sleeves make it seasonless—pair it with a cami in spring, or a cashmere Henley in winter.

Read on to see this same jacket worn three more ways, proving that you don't need to buy many pieces; you just need to buy the most versatile ones.

Bright Idea

By tucking her jeans into her boots, trading the sweater for a black T-shirt, and throwing on a cobalt blue scarf, Annique can get ready for a fashionable dinner with friends downtown. "It's amazing how much of a difference the right colorful accessory makes," she says. See how sporty the jacket looks styled this way?

CASUAL WORKING LUNCH

Hot Rocks

"I begged Jesse, 'Listen, you have to tell women what to wear on a date!' You don't want to look like you're trying too hard. You want to be sexy, but not so sexy that you're sending the wrong message. I need an outfit that's flirty but still serious enough that it's not like, 'I want to go to bed with you right now.'" So, there you have it. Annique wanted to know what to wear when she asks a guy to accompany her to a high-profile event. The skinny black bones of this outfit—long knit top and superskinny jeans—show off a body Annique has worked hard for. The obi-style wraparound belt adds a fashionista's edge and highlights both her waist and her bust. The short jacket keeps the whole thing from looking too tight, and the peep-toe heels project confidence and sass. Who wouldn't want to be seen with this woman?

ACCESSORY MEMO:

When heading out for the evening, consider carrying an oversize clutch instead of a shoulder bag. This will give you a more elegant posture as you walk around with your date; you won't be slumped to one side, continually readjusting your strap.

THAT EVER-ELUSIVE "EDGE"

When we say a look "needs an edge," we mean it lacks strength or personality—it's just a little bit blah. Adding just one special accessory—in this case, a rock-and-roll clutch—can take a look from forgettable to memorable. This clutch works for someone with Annique's chic style because, despite its punky accoutrements, its silhouette is clean and classic.

Experience Under Her Belt

Underneath this artfully wrapped jacket is a simple knit top, ideal for teaching. But come evening, when Annique is going straight to a fund-raiser, all she needs to do is throw on this jacket and belt, and she's out the door. "I want to break into the nonprofit world, meet people, network—and this is the perfect look to do it in."

72

STYLING MEMO:

Just because a jacket has buttons doesn't mean you have to button it. By closing this jacket with the obi belt, we've given it a totally new, crossover look.

From the
Desk of Darcy

Because Annique didn't grow up wearing makeup, she needed to learn the ABCs of a basic face. Here's a crash course:

A. Start with clean, well-moisturized skin. Apply a thin dusting of mineral powder foundation to even skin tone.

B. Curl your eyelashes and apply two coats of volumizing mascara, working the color into the roots. This eliminates the need for separate eyeliner and makes the eyes look wide open.

C. Brighten cheeks and lips with a cream blusher, then slick on some clear lip gloss.

Voilà! A perfect face in less time than it takes to sing your ABCs.

MAKEUP MUST-HAVES: YOUR BEAUTY SHOPPING LIST

Of course, every woman's beauty needs are different, but these items will get anyone through the work day looking polished.

Tinted moisturizer
to even skin tone.

Cream-on blusher
to make you look refreshed, even when you're anything but.

Mineral powder compact
for touch-ups throughout the day.

Water-resistant mascara
to define lashes and resist running.

Neutral eye shadows with a hint of shimmer—apply lightly for day, more intensely for nighttime.

Brow defining pencil
to fill in any sparse spots.

Powder bronzer
to fake a vacation.

Sheer lip gloss
to make your lips look their fullest.

Jane, 30
The World Traveler

CAREER: Travel consultant and chief financial officer

BASELINE WORKSTYLE: Kooky Gal

WORKSONALITY: The Director

WORKPLACE: Casual

STYLETYPE: Whimsical Chic

COLORTYPE: Earth 🌍

The Challenge:
To unite a closet full of incredible pieces; to set the fashion bar in a family-owned business

The Baseline:
Jane's go-to dress is a deep-aqua trapeze style. "It's asymmetrical and loose fitting, comfortable and easy," she says. "It makes me feel relaxed but put-together at the same time. Sometimes I belt it, which gives it a different feel. It is really a simple piece, but I can accessorize it to make it look a bit more interesting." Nothing wrong with this look—it communicates ease, comfort, and fashion confidence. Still, since Jane was looking for a bit more polish, we wanted to make an effort to introduce her to shapes that fit closer to the body.

Jane is a lifelong downtown girl—and it shows in her style. "When I was growing up, hip-hop was just beginning—there was so much going on. Our neighborhood was a true cross-section. I always had the freedom to dress creatively, and my family gave me the autonomy to express who I wanted to be." This meant collecting vintage pieces, mixing designer things with inexpensive ones, and featuring the occasional heirloom piece from her Italian grandmother or her Jamaican mom.

In fact, Jane's mother, Rose, and her Aunt Jolly are her fashion inspirations; she looks to photos of them living in London during their twenties whenever she needs ideas. "They were very free-spirited—so inspiring, fresh, and current. My mom thinks the way I dress now is rather conservative, actually!"

With all due respect to Jane's mom, most people wouldn't agree: Jane's wardrobe is a well-curated treasure trove. We were practically drooling over many of the things we found in her closet, from the ceremonial necklace she picked up in Africa to her collection of serious statement shoes. Jane is the rare woman who needs no help seeking out unique items that represent her style. She came to us looking for advice on how to put the pieces of her collection together into complete looks, in order to project the competency and authority she aims for as a Director.

Jane works in her family business—a luxury travel agency founded and owned by her mother—along with her brother and other family members. "It can be challenging spending all day with your family. Everything plays out on the office stage." Jane's office stage includes bona fide stars, too: the agency caters to VIPs, varying from foreign dignitaries to hip-hop artists to supermodels, so Jane needs to look professional *and* current. Since she spends most of her day sitting at a desk, though, she needs fabrics that resist wrinkling and shapes that don't constrict or stretch out. "I love the look of body-conscious clothing, but I'm a little more comfortable in something that's not." She's also looking to grow up her look a bit, having recently hit an age milestone. "I want to wear stuff that's body conscious while I still have a body—I went through a lot, turning thirty!—but I'd also like to look a little bit more adult. Working with your family is so, well, *familiar;* it's important to dress in a way that you're respected."

In order to keep her edge while simplifying and streamlining her look a bit, we encouraged Jane to embrace her dress-a-day philosophy. *Dress-a-day* means just what it sounds like—it's a radically simplified way to approach clothing because you don't need to buy pants, skirts, or tops! "Wearing a dress is the easiest thing. It's just one piece, all-encompassing; all you have to do is choose your bag and shoes, and you're out the door."

Jacket Required

Is it just us, or does Jane look like she went from a size 8 to a size 6 by simply switching from a tent dress to something tailored? As much as we love the strong statement volume makes, sometimes drapey dresses can overwhelm a small frame like Jane's. This combination of sleek sheath, jacket, and boots does just the opposite, giving her a strong, powerful, urban look. "This outfit made me feel more adult as I am coming out of my twenties and moving into my thirties, trying to acquire a more mature and respectable look. Sometimes I don't like to attract too much attention, so I gravitate toward a neutral palette. Also, the shape of the neckline accented my necklace, which I love."

STYLING MEMO:

If you have a statement jewelry piece, such as this Ethiopian wedding necklace that Jane picked up while studying abroad in Zimbabwe, pair it with clean lines and don't be afraid to hide it a little (notice the way Jane wears hers). There's no better way to get people interested in something than to conceal it!

76

Dress and Tie

This body-skimming wool dress has a bit of a 1920s feel but doesn't read at all retro, because of its sleek execution and gorgeous fabric. "I really like the tie detail—I think it looks professional but also stylish and avant-garde. This is me going for a more polished look, while staying funky, young, and interesting." Worn without tights and with statement shoes in brown, rather than a more traditional black pair, this dress is the perfect piece to transition into fall. The orange bag provides a fun, fashionable contrast to the outfit's palette—a pop! You'll hear us say it a hundred times, but don't be afraid of bright accessories.

From the
Desk of Darcy

Since Jane takes fashion inspiration from all the exotic locales she visits, I encouraged her to take beauty cues as well. I showed her how to smudge a kohl *kajal* natural eye pencil—popular in parts of Europe and the Middle East—into her lash lines to play up her eyes' almond shape.

QUICK-CHANGE MEMO:

Don't forget about brown. Brown leather shoes—like the chunky ankle-strap platforms we've chosen here—have a timeless feel and go just as well as black shoes would with most things.

Shine It Up

For Jane, stepping it up a notch means taking her signature neutral dress and adding some sparkle. "I would need to be going to an event after work to wear something like this, but I really did love it. I felt very powerful, very much my age, very in charge." Spoken like a true Director! Notice that we chose a neutral belt instead of a black one in order not to break the line of the dress. Black tights and burgundy suede shoes gave what could have been a very country-club vibe a downtown flavor.

QUICK-CHANGE MEMO:

If you have to go straight to an event from the office but are worried that the dress you want to wear is a little too much for the workday, wear boots and a long sweater during the day, then leave them in your office when it's time to go to the party.

Oh, Happy Day

Jane has always loved to wear vintage, and, since her style icons are the 1970s versions of her mom and aunt, we chose this red paisley dress from the same decade. It's amazing how current some vintage designs can be, isn't it? This dress wouldn't be out of place on a rack at Bergdorf's today. "It's not obvious in the photo, but this dress has maybe twelve buttons that go up the sleeves—I love that detail. I use the trick of wearing a big belt with a lot of my looser dresses—it can make two different dresses out of one."

Rebecca, late 30s

The Glamorous Work-from-Home Mom

CAREER: Freelance writer and editor

BASELINE WORKSTYLE:
Ms. Casual Friday

WORKSONALITY: The Independent

WORKPLACE: Public, Home Office

STYLETYPE: Bohemian Chic

COLORTYPE: Earth

The Challenge:

To help a stay-at-home mom move effortlessly back and forth between the computer, the playroom, and the outside world

The Baseline:

Here's mother and daughter in matching fisherman's sweaters, ready for a day on the town. ("I swear, I don't usually dress us alike!" she says. We say, "Why not?") This is the kind of thing Rebecca wears in both her personal and professional life. There's nothing wrong with it, but Rebecca wants to embrace a more structured, more motivating look.

Few job transitions are more dramatic than going from freelance journalist to stay-at-home mom. "I used to be such a go-go girl," says Rebecca, who had her daughter, Nina, just over a year ago. "I was always on the go. Motherhood has given me focus but not on my looks. I want to develop a look that works and that can be easily converted for meetings and a playdate." Now that Rebecca is easing back into journalism, she needs a wardrobe that will communicate instant professionalism while also remaining functional when she's at home with her daughter.

Rebecca worked as a model for years and has a strong appreciation for unusual, high-design pieces; we wanted her wardrobe to reflect that. It may sound easy to incorporate drama into your look when you're almost six feet tall and a sample size, but the challenge is to make sure nothing looks mismatched or haphazard. "In my real life, I'm vintage-y and casual, so I've always had to strive to look a little more professional."

Like many women who work from home, Rebecca has become accustomed to wearing stay-at-home-mom chic: leggings and a knit dress, or jeans and a T-shirt. "This makes me feel relaxed and ready to hit the floor with my one-year-old or run to the café for a coffee and e-mail." But now that her career is ramping up again, Rebecca needs ensembles she can wear outside her inner sanctum. We wanted to outfit her with everything she needs to impress a journalistic source or a future client—and give her the confidence to be a true Independent.

The New Multitasker

Here's our take on updating Rebecca's go-anywhere outfit. In it, she can still move around easily in order to take care of her daughter, but she could also run down to City Hall to do document research or meet for a casual check-in lunch with a client. This is the ideal look when Rebecca wants to fly under the radar, especially when thrown into a situation with other journalists. "In Chicago, journalistic style is old school. People wear wrinkled shirts and pleated khakis. If you're too fashionable, your credibility can go out the window."

COLOR MEMO:

For some reason, many people relegate themselves to wearing brown with khaki and gray with black. But we love brown and gray together—there's something in the contrast between the earthy neutral and the steely noncolor that feels fresh and sophisticated. The lesson? Don't follow any prescriptive "rules" when it comes to combining colors. Look in the mirror, and trust your gut.

Getting the Scoop

Here's Rebecca looking beautiful in browns again, this time in a *His Girl Friday*-inspired look that will take her to interview local politicians or VIPs, and then out to a grown-up drink with her husband. "I love earthy colors," she says. "It's easier to make them look interesting. And black is too harsh for my coloring." Rebecca also loved the mix of finishes and textures in this look. "I like the soft suit with textured tights, contrasting with the shiny shoes and bag. I've always liked combining two sides of the spectrum—rock and roll meets conservative, or high and low mixed. It's better than pretty and perfect." We couldn't agree more.

ACCESSORY MEMO:

Look for handbags with a couple of carrying options. Rebecca is holding onto this slouchy tote by its bracelet handle, but if her arm gets tired, she can sling the long strap over her shoulder. This is especially important when she needs to scoop up the baby in addition to her handbag.

SHOPPING MEMO:

We found this luxurious look at a consignment shop for a fraction of its original price. Don't be afraid to shop in secondhand stores; women who buy high fashion shop seasonally, and so much of the clothing they donate is barely worn and less than a year old.

Warm Reception

Says Rebecca, "This is a creative and fashion-y look. Wide-leg pants make sense in the business world—business people don't understand skinny pants!"

From the
Desk of Darcy

When you're a new mom like Rebecca, you don't have time for much of a routine. The key is to conceal under-eye circles and brighten a tired skin tone. I chose a matte mousse foundation for Rebecca and applied it as I would concealer, just to the areas where she needed it. I made sure her brows were well groomed and defined, then gave her some lip balm and she was good to go.

The Challenge:

To add depth and sophistication to a flighty wardrobe and create looks that will help take Amanda through a long day at the office and multiple events

The Baseline:

This is Amanda's favorite outfit. But worn as a dress, this Missoni piece is less than flattering: its wavy horizontal pattern is widening rather than elongating, and its coloration draws the eye directly to the hips, the widest point on the body. We liked the piece, but we knew she could wear it better.

Amanda, 38

The Show Girl

CAREER: Public relations and marketing executive

BASELINE WORKSTYLE:
Kooky Gal

WORKSONALITY: The Muse

WORKPLACE: Creative

STYLETYPE: Whimsical

COLORTYPE: Earth 🌐

With a spectacular career in fashion PR, it's no surprise Amanda has what we in the fashion industry like to call a major point of view. There's nothing wishy-washy or ambivalent about the rows and rows of sparkle and shine we found in her closet. "I'm no stranger to glitter in daytime," Amanda says. But, while we love a risk-taker, a woman with a job as powerful as Amanda's can't survive on frosting alone—even the über-Muse needs some cake, too.

There are few people for whom a metallic, knit, printed cardigan/dress would be considered *practical*, but Amanda is one of them. We're the first to admit that, since she goes to an event nearly every night of the week, statement pieces are a matter of necessity for this It-Girl. But we wanted to help her develop her wardrobe a bit, to fill in some holes left by all the fairy-princess fantasy pieces she's collected over the years. We wanted to take her from Carrie Bradshaw to Sarah Jessica Parker.

WARDROBE WISDOM:

They're accessories, not excessories. Any one of the pieces Amanda is sporting here would be amazing on its own—against a more neutral backdrop. Worn altogether, they're too much.

Open for Business

Voilà! Same cardigan, totally different look. Worn open, over a sleek tank and trousers, the piece goes from baby-doll to hot mama. The pattern no longer draws attention to any trouble spots—it simply adds interest to what would otherwise be a neutral ensemble. And when the cardigan is worn open, the fabric can drape easily, creating a fluid and flattering back view. Also notice how toning down the accessories brings everything down to a chic simmer.

FIGURE MEMO:

It's tempting to try to camouflage the parts we're not proudest of with long, loose tunic tops and sweaters. Do us a favor and try a long cardigan worn open over sleek pieces instead. You'll get the same coverage on the back and sides of your body, but showing your waist and some décolletage will keep the look feminine and flattering, not frumpy.

Cozy Casual

On the rare day that Amanda has no nighttime event to attend, she can get things done in a monochromatic look that reads sophisticated and well thought out but is as comfortable as sweats. "I like how these pieces are not the same exact color, but they work well together. Some people might think this is a lot of bundling up for work, but Chicago is absolutely freezing in the wintertime," Amanda says.

WARDROBE WISDOM:

If you live in a warm climate or are simply hot blooded, you can get this same look by choosing a long-sleeved knit in a hue from your Colortype palette.

Black Magic

Sometimes wearing all black can make a woman look—and feel—as though she's on her way to a funeral, the last thing you want when you're on your way to a party! Worn on its own, this cowl-neck black dress would be appropriate for the most somber of situations. But we wanted to loosen it up, so we layered in off-white pops. The bracelets make the outfit less severe. A black dress with an off-white shoe is unexpected, making a bold and chic statement.

STYLING MEMO:

Notice how, even though we popped the outfit with off-white accessories, we chose to pair the dress with a black belt. Not only is this more flattering than an off-white one, but it also seems cooler and less studied than match-ing belt and shoes.

SHOWSTOPPING SHOES

Afraid to step out in dramatic foot-wear? Let these incredible pairs serve as inspiration. Even though they're all a bit wild, these styles are completely versatile. And even though they're super-high, their platforms make them totally wearable.

The Real Teal

Before her current stint in PR, Amanda hosted a television show about fine dining and also managed a popular restaurant—so she's a real fixture on the social circuit. Hence, she's used to being photographed. A lot. This look would be a great choice for the red carpet because of its balance between vibrant color and glowing skin, and the way each plays off the other. Also note the careful choice of accessories. Her gold snakeskin disco shoes and long gold necklace riff off one another and give the look a festive feel without being overpowering. A Muse wants to inspire, not overwhelm.

86

From the
Desk of Darcy

A true showgirl always knows her light—and for Amanda, this means adding shimmer and sparkle to create drama when she goes from daytime to evening. She can do this by applying a luminescent eye shadow to her eyelids and a shimmer gloss on top of her lipstick.

YOU OUGHT TO BE IN PICTURES

HOW TO LOOK YOUR BEST IN PHOTOGRAPHS

Not all of us pose for a living. Consequently, we're not hip to the insider tricks. But here's the information we've gleaned from our photographer friends over the years:

Wear color—not black—near your face.

In general, choose solid colors over patterns. Small patterns can be okay, but big ones will distract from your face.

Don't show too much skin.

Unless you're on the thin side, avoid shiny fabrics.

Wear light-reflecting earrings.

Never face the camera head-on: Turn your body the slightest bit to the side, and then turn your head to look at the camera. This will make you look narrower.

Take a deep breath, exhale, and relax your chest to elongate your neck.

Press your tongue up against the roof of your mouth to minimize a double chin. You can also try tilting your chin down a bit and looking up at the camera.

Throw your shoulders back and put a hand on one hip to slim your waist.

Wear sheer lip gloss rather than dark lipstick. This will make your lips look full and won't draw attention to teeth that aren't perfectly white.

Avoid sparkly eye shadow, which will look totally disco in a flash photo.

Blot your face with a tissue to matte any perspiration or oil.

Think about something that truly makes you happy. This will help you avoid the tight, nervous smile that makes looking at some wedding photos so uncomfortable.

Alex, 39

The Super Mom

CAREER: Assistant director of membership and registration, New York Jewish Community Center

BASELINE WORKSTYLE: Ms. Casual Friday

WORKSONALITY: The Director

WORKPLACE: Public

STYLETYPE: Classic Chic

COLORTYPE: Star ☆

The Challenge:

To create a look that projects warmth and authority; to help a single mom feel special, even when she's stretched too thin

The Baseline:

Alex bought this scoop-neck T-shirt in a variety of colors; it was inexpensive and easy to launder, and she knew she'd get a lot of use out of it. While we applaud her on the color choice—blue enhances her amazing eyes—we think wearing a knit without a jacket is too casual for someone in a management position. The gray pants she's wearing are fine for a basic, but they don't fit her properly in the rise, and their loose, masculine leg shape does little to show off her curvy figure. Most important, this outfit doesn't project the sense of authority a Director must exude.

With a nine-year-old daughter and a job managing twenty people under the age of thirty at a popular Jewish Community Center, Alex sometimes feels like she's everybody's mom. Her everyday wardrobe reflects this image of herself—it's practical, functional, and made to fade into the background, letting others take center stage. We wanted to remind Alex that she's a vivacious young woman and that highlighting certain elements of her femininity can only work in her favor.

Alex recently received a big promotion, and she wants to project authority and confidence in her new role. "I'm not a micro-manager," she explains. "I want my employees to see me as someone who gives them the tools they need. I support them, not the other way around." As you can see, this woman is just a tad *too* selfless. We wanted to help her find her spunk.

In addition to injecting excitement into her wardrobe, another priority was to give Alex a few items she can wear many different ways. A single mom has lots of expenses, so Alex needs things that she can get serious use out of and that don't require a ton of cash to maintain (dry cleaning really adds up).

Woven Together

Here's a more sophisticated version of the same outfit: It's amazing what a woven shirt (rather than a knit one) and pants that fit can do. These charcoal wool trousers are a nice update to the cotton ones Alex wore to our shoot; their fabric has body and stretch and their leg shape starts out close fitting and then widens a bit to elongate her legs. With the new silhouette we gave her, she looks like she lost 15 pounds; she's a size 10, but she looks like a size 6.

WARDROBE WISDOM:

Charcoal is our favorite neutral for bottoms. It goes with every color and magically tends to make whatever it's worn with look expensive.

Trailblazer

Adding a pin-striped jacket to the trousers from the previous photograph takes Alex's look to a new level—almost like a make-your-own power suit. "This jacket would be perfect in transitional weather," Alex says. "I could remove it when sitting at my desk and throw it on to go to a meeting with my boss." Although Alex normally doesn't like pockets on her jackets, we showed her that the diagonal placement of these flap pockets actually creates a slimming line. Finishing off the look are pointy-toed pumps in the same color as her pants to lengthen her leg lines.

POP MEMO:

You'll notice we've popped all Alex's looks with shades of berry and purple. If you have limited time to get ready in the morning, choose one family of pop colors and stick to it. This way, you can grab a top and bottom blindfolded (or while making your daughter's lunch), and you're out the door.

SHOPPING MEMO:

Shopping secondhand? Read this first.

This is another look with more dash than cash. We scored Alex's jacket at a resale shop—never worn, $20. And her designer heels came from a flea market, also never worn, for $10.

We cannot stress enough how not-embarrassed you should be to score other people's castoffs. First of all, used is the greenest way to shop—everything is 100 percent recycled! And of course you can score ridiculous deals. Clothes are just like new cars—once you drive them off the lot, they lose most of their resale value, but none of their quality.

A gray flannel pinstripe suit is an ideal secondhand purchase because of its classic style and fabric. We especially liked this one because of its two-button, fitted jacket and straight-leg pants; it's an ideal balance between masculine and feminine. When shopping for a gently-used suit, consider the following: The fabric should be smooth, not pilly. It should smell fresh; not like mothballs, or its previous owner. The lining should be smoothly sewn, with no holes, and made of silk. Finally, make sure you like each piece on its own as well as part of the suit. You'll get more wear out of the jacket and trousers as separates.

Used shoes are a bit tougher to buy, but finding great ones can be an amazing score. These Charles Jourdan pumps would retail for $300 or more but we paid just $10 for them. When considering secondhand shoes, make sure the leather or suede has no rips or tears (scuffs on leather can be covered by polish), and that their shape is intact, not stretched out.

It's All in the Jeans

Alex has never had a pair of updated, dark denim jeans; we wanted to show her how versatile and flattering they can be. Layered over a perfect basic foundation, the rich burgundy wrap Alex is rocking here is a dramatic and luxurious surprise. Just as we did with the gray trousers, we matched Alex's shoe color to her pants in order to elongate her legs. And, of course, the soft heather gray turtleneck will work just as well with her gray trousers and pin-striped jacket. It's great when all the items in your closet are friends.

That's a Wrap

When Alex came out in this deep aubergine wrap dress, her daughter Leila burst into happy tears. "My daughter doesn't normally see me looking feminine. Her jaw dropped," Alex says. We wanted to give Alex a magical look. This dress represents a reinvigoration of her feminine side—after initially wearing the trousers in the family for the last ten years raising her daughter—and is perfect for a fund-raising event at work. Its deep-V and wrap style show off her waist and décolletage, and its just-below-the-knee length is comfortable yet still emphasizes her shapely calves.

From the
Desk of Darcy

Many women with beautiful olive complexions like Alex's choose concealer that's too light for their skin tone. Your concealer should match your foundation so you don't look like you've been skiing with sunglasses.

Charlotte, 40
The Biz Whiz

CAREER: Entrepreneur

BASELINE WORKSTYLE:
Ms. Casual Friday

WORKSONALITY: The Independent

WORKPLACE: Public, Home Office

STYLETYPE: Classic

COLORTYPE: Earth 🌍

The Challenge:
To help a techie tomboy impress New York fashion people, and create a stylish, on-the-go wardrobe that's as comfortable as anything you could buy at Niketown

The Baseline:
We found it hard to believe that people were willing to give Charlotte millions of dollars when she was dressed for a step class, but that's Silicon Valley for you. It's true that Charlotte has an innate sense of how to show off her physique—notice that her yoga pants are slim and straight, her jacket is strategically color-blocked and body conscious—but we couldn't wait to show her how incredible she'd look in "real" clothes.

When you've lived in as many cities as Charlotte has, you become a bit of a chameleon. From San Francisco to Seattle, Boston to Los Angeles, she's covered many of our country's major metropolitan areas, and she's always dressed the part. Her Silicon Valley wardrobe was casual and crunchy; she added some fleece in honor of her move to Seattle. In Boston, she was preppy and conservative; the Los Angeles sun brought out her flirty side. But now, after starting and selling successful companies all over the country, Charlotte's gearing up to launch her next venture in New York City—and she needs to look the part. Not only because New York is the chicest city in the country, but also because her next project is all about fashion.

"I have worked in technology for many, many years—no matter how hard I try and get out of it, it keeps pulling me back!" Charlotte says. Charlotte's talent is organizing data, and although she's focused on numbers and arcane information for years, now she's looking to organize people's wardrobes online. Her new company—covetedcloset .com—aims to give women a virtual catalog of every piece of clothing and accessory they own so they can better plan their outfits and shop with ease. With all Charlotte's experience in designing software, figuring out how to organize and display this information is easy—but knowing how to present herself as she seeks funding for her new company is not. "The hard part for me is that I'm not of the fashion world," she says. "I'm of the tech world and the business world, but my audience for getting funded is not the tech route—it's the media execs and folks in fashion. I have two degrees from Harvard, and I can figure out any math problem. But if you ask me to explain why this should be purple and not red, I'm stumped," she says. We were happy to give this genius some operating instructions for her own closet.

Charlotte is a vivacious triathlete who's game for showing off her bod and taking smart fashion risks—the picture of a true Independent. Our goal was to help her recognize what she likes about her sporty West Coast wardrobe and then seek some of those same qualities in her sleek New York pieces.

Jeanius

Here, Charlotte proves that jeans don't have to be sloppy. Paired with a deep chocolate wrap top, a textured brown blazer, and brown suede boots, dark denim looks sophisticated and purposeful. We also switched her nylon laptop bag for a chic, shiny carryall—the only people who should be carrying schoolbags are schoolchildren.

LAPTOP MEMO:

When choosing a tote to carry your computer, ask the salesperson to show you how the bag handles something heavy. After you place the item in the bag—a sales manual or a phone book works well—notice how well the bag's handles and lining deal with stress and weight. If you notice any pulling or tension, put the bag back on the shelf. Otherwise, you risk being stuck between meetings with a broken handle or, worse, a broken laptop.

SCORING A STATUS BAG (WITHOUT PAYING RETAIL)

Charlotte's Marni bag is key to her powerful, sophisticated look, but most of us can't afford to drop a couple grand on a purse. Here are the top 5 ways to get a status bag for a song:

1 Check eBay for lightly used handbags. If you're not sure of authenticity, go to the designer's store and examine the real version before you buy.

2 Visit bagborroworsteal.com, or other accessory-lending Web sites. For a monthly membership fee, you can borrow some of the most expensive bags in the world. It's Netflix for purses.

3 Visit thrift or consignment shops affiliated with highbrow charities, especially ones in high-end neighborhoods. Oftentimes socialites donate their used items to charities they support—and those just around the corner from where they live.

4 Become a member of online sample sale Web sites such as gilt.com and hautelook.com, which offer off-season items at a steep discount.

5 Hit department stores' end-of-season sales. For a few days, many items can be discounted as deeply as 80 percent. Some stores even "pre-sale" items, which means you pay the sale price before the item is marked down, then pick it up once the sale starts. Don't be too shy to ask a salesperson about this.

94

No Jacket Required

This look couldn't be simpler—but its proportions are perfect. The jacket's high neck, curved collar, and puffy sleeves draw attention to Charlotte's dainty frame. And notice the Cartier watch, which, even when worn with a low-key outfit like this one, conveys wealth and sophistication (a must when you're asking people to let you take care of their money). "I am usually a fan of what I call little toy watches—you know, Timex and Nike—because I work out a lot. But recently a friend told me that they weren't cutting it anymore. I asked Jesse and Joe, 'Do people really notice such a small detail?' And they were like, 'If you have one, then you look to see whether others do, too. It's like a secret club. The people who have money to give away have nice watches.' So, I've decided that when I get funding, I'll buy one. Hopefully, it won't be too late!"

The New Power Suit

One of the biggest challenges Independents like Charlotte face is to figure out how to convey power in a feminine, but not overly sexy or domineering, way. We think the way to accomplish this is by donning a slim but shaped suit that fits your body like a glove. This deep-green number includes a sleek pencil skirt and a fit-and-flare peplum jacket, which adds a touch of softness. Because the top is a hybrid between a shirt and a jacket, there's no need for an under layer, so bringing it on a long-distance business trip couldn't be easier. "I don't usually wear the shape of this jacket," Charlotte says. "But I liked it so much, I wanted to buy it."

Like Buttah

Leather isn't just for outerwear—soft, lightweight varieties work well as blazers and cropped jackets, too. This jacket's short length, abbreviated sleeves, and volume-creating pleats at the neckline make it a good choice for Charlotte's shape; it has body without overwhelming her small frame. "I don't usually wear cropped jackets," Charlotte says. "But that's because I didn't know what to wear under them." The secret? Don't look for a short top; this silhouette is designed to let the underpinning peek out.

96

Dressed for Success

Gone are the days when women needed to dress like the female version of Gordon Gekko from the movie *Wall Street* in order to nail a presentation. This softly patterned dress paired with a cardigan would be equally at home in a boardroom and a dining room. "An outfit that makes you feel like a million bucks makes you feel like you can raise a million bucks," Charlotte says. We gave this look even more personality by pairing it with tights and pumps in deep chocolate brown rather than the more mundane black you might expect.

From the
Desk of Darcy

Charlotte is streamlined, from her chic bob to her compact shape. I wanted to give her a streamlined makeup wardrobe as well, so I applied eye, lip, and cheek colors all in plum shades from the same palette. When in doubt, go monochromatic.

STYLE COUNSEL
Martha McCully

As the founding beauty director of *Allure* magazine and the longtime executive editor of *InStyle,* Martha McCully knows what it takes to dress for success. As a judge on HGTV's *Design Star,* she has learned to articulate her opinions.

When you interview a woman for a position, are there signs of grooming and dressing that you look for?

Yes. I want to see someone who is clean, neat, and finding solutions to her grooming and wardrobe issues. If you have unruly hair, tame it; if you don't have a perfect body, find the clothes that flatter what you have; if you have breakouts, don't wear heavy makeup. Nothing is worse in an interview than focusing on the interviewee's hair in her eyes, pink eye shadow, or halter top.

Are there any red flags—wardrobe-wise—that make you worry about hiring someone?

Absolutely. I never understand when someone wears underwear as outerwear to an interview. I would say spaghetti straps, tube tops, flesh-colored slips all turn me off. So does "nightclub wear," like supershort dresses or things that are too sparkly. Chipped nail polish, open-toe sandals when a pedicure is needed—you get the picture. Anything that I can't stop looking at during the interview and thinking, "What was she thinking?" One woman I interviewed I really liked, but I wouldn't hire her because she wore too much perfume.

How important is it to dress for work? Is it better to be overdressed or underdressed?

Obviously, it depends on what business you are in. If it's an image business, where appearance counts, then be conscious of the fact that you send a message with your wardrobe choices. Underdressed never works for me (see above). Even Fridays—I don't think I've ever worn jeans to work. Overdressing is tricky, too. You can wear hints of cocktail attire if they're toned down with something very professional. But don't go overboard on the nighttime, sexy attire during the day, it's just distracting and sends a weird message.

Do you notice any similarities among women—in terms of how they present themselves—who rise up the company ladder quickly?

Women who are accomplished, or who want to be accomplished, in their professional lives usually present themselves that way. All the loose ends are tied up. If someone is messy or too casual, usually that's a reflection of how they approach their work. If it's a corporate environment, then the more pulled-together the better. Sometimes, in a very creative, casual environment, more creative wardrobe choices can work. It's mostly about the context.

Have you ever had a wardrobe crisis during your career—maybe a size change or a need to shift your image? How did you deal with it and resolve it?

I think "crisis" is a bit strong, but I have had to manage people older than I was and also enter an existing structure as a new leader. My philosophy was always the higher the heel, the higher on the masthead (or corporate ladder). Heels somehow show authority, and I definitely used them to feel confident. That and a good blowout always seem to work. Weekly manicures show professionalism, too.

In terms of presenting yourself, are there things you know now that you wish you knew at the beginning of your career?

I wish I had known not to wear pumps. Though they do exert authority (see above), they also give you bunions later on. Try to find comfy high heels, if that's not an oxymoron.

What is the best way for a woman to assert her femininity without seeming overtly sexy?

The fabrics can be more feminine but the cuts more professional. So wear a frilly chiffon top but in a classic style with a cardigan over it.

What are your top five dressing and grooming pet peeves for the office?

1. Too much perfume
2. Too revealing or sexy
3. Showing too much feet
4. Slippers
5. Trying too hard

What is your go-to work outfit—the one that makes you feel like you're going to knock everyone's socks off?

A stylist once told me to pick a movie character and then emulate her style. When I was in a corporate creative office, my style role model was Faye Dunaway in *Network*. Slinky buttoned shirts, long necklaces, slouchy pants, maybe a short jacket or a cardigan as a jacket. This also is a good way to keep you in one style and not all over the place, which just reflects a lack of focus. The main idea is to express with your wardrobe and grooming who you are, what your work style is, and that you are more serious about work than fixing your outfit all day.

Cynthia, 40s
The Multitasking Mama

CAREER: Stay-at-home mom; volunteer at the Art Institute of Chicago, the Kenwood Open House Committee, and her twin boys' Montessori school

BASELINE WORKSTYLE: Sexy Lady

WORKSONALITY: The Collaborator

WORKPLACE: Creative, Home Office

WORKSTYLE: Feminine

STYLETYPE: Whimsical Chic

COLORTYPE: Sun ☼

The Challenge:
To help a mom-of-all-trades unite all the showstoppers in her closet with a system of hard-working foundation pieces, so she can move through her life as one person—herself—instead of a series of different personalities

The Baseline:
Business as usual for Cynthia is party time for the rest of us. This fur-trimmed Etro dream coat is what Cynthia runs around the city in; it's a lot of fun, but we wanted to work toward a less embellished, more polished look for her.

One might think that quitting modeling and becoming a full-time mom would mean less fashion pressure. Not if you're Cynthia! In addition to taking care of her twin boys full-time, Cynthia serves on the boards of three different organizations and frequently attends philanthropic events and business engagements with her husband. "You've got the ladies who lunch at the Art Institute, that's one look. Then there's the mom look, and the taking-care-of-the-husband look, and the toned-down school- and neighborhood-volunteer look. I think I have all the elements to look great in every situation, but if I could find a way to scale down the differences between them and bring them together in order to make fluid transitions from one situation to another, that would make my life so much easier."

We've had the pleasure of knowing Cynthia for years. Growing up in front of the camera, Cynthia developed the sort of fearless sense of style we all covet. But it can be difficult for her to fit her Technicolor wardrobe into some of the more muted environments she finds herself in these days. When you're working to make your kids' school a better place, you want to be recognized for your ideas, not your stilettos. In a way, Cynthia is transitioning from the role of Muse to Collaborator.

"I've got fifty personalities in my head, since I was a model for so many years. I've always felt like I could get away with anything—that's what's exciting about being in the fashion industry. But now I'm not always sure people will understand my looks," Cynthia says. We wanted to streamline things for Cynthia—to maintain the va-va-voom girl but help her reinvent herself as *toned-down, sexy, and chic.*

In the Trenches

What could be more functional—and beautiful—for running from school to the grocery store to a casual meeting than a perfect black trench worn with jeans? "In the Midwest, you're in a coat practically nine months out of the year. That's what people see. I want to be able to put that fabulous coat on and feel instantly put-together," Cynthia says. This Lanvin number's slight sheen and perfect fit give it a very expensive look, and its featherweight construction means Cynthia can leave it on indoors when she wants to be in more than just jeans and a top. Cynthia is considering a second career in real estate—she just got her license—and this would be the perfect outfit in which to meet a client or show a house.

WARDROBE WISDOM:

If you want to wear jeans at night, pair them with a sheer black top, like this one by Roberto Cavalli. This look balances high and low and is perfect for situations where the dress code is ambiguous, such as an early-evening cocktail with the husband or a spontaneous casual dinner after shopping.

UNDER COVER

Knowing what to wear under a sheer top such as this one can be confusing. Is something so see-through ever appropriate? The answer is yes, as long as you're covered up underneath. We love slimming one-piece bodysuits in solid, rather than lacy, fabrics. They create a clean line and keep everything from moving around (especially for busty ladies like Cynthia).

102

The Day—or Night—Shift

You've heard of the LBD (little black dress); now meet the LND (little navy dress)! This simple piece in the most classic of colors will take Cynthia anywhere in style. "This sleeveless boatneck is my luncheon uniform—appropriate, no matter what. It's the perfect length, and it's got a little sexiness because it's got a little swing. My motto is, You've always got to have a little sexy in there," Cynthia says. We agree, but we love that this little number is sexy because of what it conceals—not what it reveals. The high boatneck glides over Cynthia's décolletage, the bias-cut skirt skims over her curves, and the hem ends at the most flattering point on her leg, just below the knee. She appears approachable, like a true Collaborator. When you're leggy and voluptuous like Cynthia, show off your limbs—they'll create the illusion that what's under the fabric is just as long and lean as what's outside it.

STYLING MEMO:

This gem is a staple in Cynthia's closet, and she wears it frequently—with a pair of pink, black, and ivory shoes that, in our opinion, are too whimsical and dilute the strong lines of the dress. We wanted to choose accessories that would rock out the outfit, making an old look new again. Platform pinup-girl pumps, a tough leather clutch, and a heavy gold-chain bracelet give the dress a cool Parisian feel.

From the Desk of Darcy

Cynthia is not afraid to have fun with makeup. I showed her how to take a smoky eye from day to evening—starting out with earthy shades in the morning, then working in plums and blacks as the sun goes down. To really be a showstopper at events, makeup lovers like Cynthia should reach for the false eyelashes.

Warm and Cozy

Nothing flatters like head-to-toe mono-chromatic dressing—it doesn't cut the body in half at the waist, so the overall effect is streamlined and slimming. Since Cynthia has long legs and a short torso, she benefits from a deep V-neck, which elongates her top half. "This is the perfect, classy, evening dress. It's pretty much a wow. I would wear it to a special event with my husband—it shows off my curves, but it's clean and classic. It's a good dress to have for ten years if you can still fit into it."

STYLING MEMO:

"Dressy" dresses can be great for daytime—if you know how to take them down a notch. This one would look great with suede boots on a fall day.

A Sexy Twist

We like to think of this look as grown-up va-va-voom. The gathering just under Cynthia's bustline draws attention to her Fellini-star proportions, and the drapey fluidness of the fabric means it glides right over her curves. The chunky grosgrain peep-toe shoes from Alberta Ferretti give the look a bit of an edge, and the metallic mock-croc clutch adds flash.

The Challenge:

To convince a woman who "doesn't like shopping," but who just married a man who "encourages [her] to spend money on clothes," that dressing well is a valid and worthwhile mode of self-expression

The Baseline:

This is Oriyan's unofficial uniform: a woven top with some interest—here, it's wrap detailing at the waist—and black pants. While this outfit gets her through the day, we wanted to remind her that clothes can be a little more fun.

Oriyan, 32
The Legal Eagle

CAREER: Attorney

BASELINE WORKSTYLE:
Lady in Uniform

WORKSONALITY: The Independent

WORKPLACE: Formal

STYLETYPE: Classic

COLORTYPE: Moon ☾

As a lawyer working mostly with fashion, entertainment, and new media clients, Oriyan lives in two distinct worlds. Her law firm is traditional, but she often works with very creative people. To dress with ease, no matter whose company she finds herself in, Oriyan has developed a uniform she wears almost every day: a pair of black pants with a cute top. But now that she's moving into her mid-thirties and recently married, she'd like to step up her look a bit.

"My husband loves me in skirts and heels, but he also realizes heels are pretty painful," Oriyan says, pointing at her flats. We wanted to show her that fashion doesn't have to be punishing. We hoped to encourage Oriyan to approach her wardrobe with the same spirit of innovation with which she approaches her work.

The first item of business was to convince her that, despite her petite height, her feminine proportions mean her body is flattered by most silhouettes. Second, we had to show her how to make the most of her curves without feeling overexposed. Finally, we gave her a vibrant tote and clutch and proved that great accessories can invigorate even the most basic outfit. As an Independent, Oriyan already has a strong sense of herself professionally, and we wanted to help her extend that confidence to her wardrobe.

The Magical Jacket

Oriyan usually stays away from jackets because she feels they make her look shorter. After trying on a number of styles, we discovered that a jacket that cuts away—one that's shorter in front and longer in back—makes her look taller. Matching her pants with her jacket is a bit too mature-looking for Oriyan, so we chose this gray sharkskin blazer because it coordinates with her favorite black pants but still provides contrast.

WARDROBE WISDOM:

Leave a special jacket like this one hanging on the back of your office door—you never know when a surprise meeting or celebration will come up.

Comfort Meets Function

For a more casual workday, Oriyan can pair her trusty black pants with a cozy cardigan and a classic white shirt. A long sweater won't look dowdy as long as it has a slim fit.

106

WARDROBE WISDOM:

Choose a sweater with an exaggerated, deep V neckline to bring attention to the décolletage and elongate the upper body.

She's Got Legs

When Oriyan told us her husband wouldn't mind seeing her look just a little bit more like a proper lady, we jumped at the chance to put her in a pencil skirt. Nothing is sexier than the hourglass silhouette created here: the slim white top accentuates her bust, and the curvy skirt highlights her legs, hitting just a couple of inches above the kneecap. Pair it with a pop-color clutch, and this look is perfect for a lunch date. Throw the gray blazer on top, and it will work in a boardroom, too.

IT'S IN THE BAG

Many women collect handbags like lipsticks, but a coordinating tote and clutch is all you really need. Carry both to work and leave the tote behind when you go out for the evening.

When shopping for a tote, look for:

An interior zipper compartment so someone can't reach in and grab your wallet

Handles long enough to fit over your shoulder, but short enough that the tote won't drag when you carry it in your hand

A cell phone pocket so you can answer—and silence—it easily

When shopping for a clutch, look for:

A size that fits comfortably under your arm, and in your hand

Enough storage space for your wallet, your phone, your keys, a lipstick, and a compact

A shape that works for both day and night

108

Subtle Elegance

There's a fine line to walk when dressing for after-hours events with superiors and colleagues: you want to look attractive but not too sexy, fashion-conscious but not trendy, dressed-up but comfortable. Jesse found this Armani dress at a vintage store, and it fit Oriyan like a glove. We paired it with chunky platform heels (she feels out of sorts in stilettos) and finished the look with an ombré wrap.

BEAUTY MEMO:

If you have to run to a formal event right after work but have just five minutes for hair and makeup, pull your hair up and away from your face, put on some earrings, and curl your lashes.

From the
Desk of Darcy

Oriyan's whole look changed when we gave her chic eyeglasses that defined her eyes instead of just disappearing into her face. Even more important, her new Robert Marc glasses came complete with no-glare lenses, which allow for direct eye contact. And don't forget: Even people who live their lives behind glasses need eye makeup. Some people are afraid that a magnified lens makes makeup look too severe, but the key is keeping things light. If you wear nothing else, choose a black mascara that defines the perimeters of your eyes. No more hiding behind those glasses!

The Challenge:

To show a busy mom and career woman that making interesting fashion choices is just as easy as making boring ones

The Baseline:

This traditional look suits Ami well. The shirtwaist dress fits her perfectly, and the belt draws attention to her slim waist—but it's too dark for her fun personality. For many Classic gals, the all-black uniform becomes a safety zone that prevents them from experimenting with color. We wanted to give Ami the opportunity to brighten up.

Ami, 32
The Scientist

CAREER: Supply-chain engineer at a pharmaceutical company, and mom

BASELINE WORKSTYLE: Ms. Mousy

WORKSONALITY: The Independent

WORKPLACE: Impersonal

STYLETYPE: Classic Chic

COLORTYPE: Star ☆

An engineer by trade, Ami Vora works with a lot of men—and she has always dressed in order not to call attention to herself. "My style hasn't really changed over the years. It's basic: slacks and a blouse is easy. I don't work downtown; I'm in a manufacturing environment, so it's easy not to make fashion a huge priority. But I've recently realized how much I want to look put-together. You exude confidence when you feel put-together."

In a business-casual environment like Ami's, where everyone is hiding in khakis and polos, it's easy to disappear. But when we met Ami, she told us that she had a strong desire to bring the stylish sensibility she shows in her personal life into her work life, too. At dinner with her husband, she might take a fashion risk in a sexy dress or sky-high heels. But at work, she was in a rut, wearing the same trousers-and-top ensemble every day. She wanted to learn how to spice things up a bit and how to incorporate color into her wardrobe. "I want to be perceived as classy but low-maintenance—not a woman who is spending three hours to get ready," she told us. With two small children, Ami is really limited in time. Our goal was to show her how easy it would be to make a few simple switches so that the key pieces in her closet would be not only functional but also fun and flattering—and so that her Independent spirit would be as evident in her clothing as it is in her personality.

Deep Purple

"I'm usually all about black," Ami says. "But I was shocked by how good the purple dress looked on my skin color!" We were inspired to find a piece to go with Ami's spectacular purple, patent handbag, which was a 10th-anniversary gift from her husband. Despite being vibrant, this look is very versatile: Ami can switch out the high-heeled boots for flat ones in order to run around with her kids, or slip on a long-sleeved T-shirt under the dress when it gets cold.

STYLING MEMO:

You don't need to fasten all belts tight around your waist. With a knit dress like this one, it can be fun and flattering to keep things a bit slouchier.

Smoky eyes and pale lips have been a classic look since the dawn of civilization, so it's no wonder they remain a favorite of many women—including Ami. You can build a great day-to-night look on this concept.

Daytime: A deep lapis blue liner brightens the whites of her eyes. Smoky, slate gray shadow brings depth to her lids, and a soft lavender keeps things light toward the brow bone. Lips are peachy pink and creamy with a touch of gloss.

Nighttime: Adding a shimmer shadow above the brows, on the inner corners of the eyes, and on top of the cheekbones adds drama. A touch of raspberry pink blush on the apples of Ami's cheeks freshens the look.

BEAUTY MEMO:

Gloss is a great choice for everyone—especially women with thinner lips. And because its color is sheer and subtle, it's a great choice for the office. Just be sure not to get too sticky!

In the Pink

Because she's a mom on the go, we wanted to give Ami another day-to-night look—as well as show her how vibrant color can make a simple silhouette look truly special. This wrap top has classic styling, but its hue takes it over the top. The most contemporary way to wear jeans is to pair them with items that are much less casual, leading to a relaxed yet polished look. Here's a good rule for how to wear denim to work: everything you wear with the denim should work just as well with dressier items, such as skirts or trousers.

UNDER COVER

Busty gals can slip a camisole under this top for coverage.

Pencil Sharp

Many women are terrified that high-waisted skirts will draw attention to their bellies. But a high waist actually elongates the body, and a high-tech knit fabric slims the waistline. "It actually hid my pouch a little!" Ami says. "I think I'm finally learning that wearing tailored clothing makes you look thinner as opposed to wearing baggy clothing, which makes you look like you're hiding in a sack. Wearing clothes that fit you means you exude confidence."

From the
Desk of Darcy

Women, like Ami, who are not accustomed to showing a bit of (appropriate) skin during the day sometimes forget to enhance the skin tone on their arms and legs. Moisturize after showering, and apply a bit of shimmer oil to arms and legs for a refined sexiness.

SKIN: HOW MUCH IS TOO MUCH?

Sometimes it's hard to know just how bare you can go at the office. For your convenience, we have developed the following simple guidelines we like to call The Seven Deadly Sins of Overexposure:

1 No shirt, no shoes, no service. If you can wear it at the beach, you shouldn't wear it at the office. This includes shorts.

2 They call it "underwear" for a reason. It is never okay to show your lingerie in a professional environment, unless you work at a bar. Actually, it's probably an even worse idea in that case.

3 If you can see the thigh, it's too high. Skirts that reveal leg above the top of the kneecap should be worn with tights.

4 Convertible bras are made specifically for risqué necklines. Therefore, no piece of work attire should require them.

5 Show the world your armpits only if they're flawless. Leave the "natural" look to the Europeans, and always bring a cardigan or jacket to cover up in case of emergency.

6 Leave the stripper shoes to the working girls—not the ones in your office.

7 No butt cleavage. These words should not even enter into your vocabulary. In fact, we're embarrassed to even have them in this book. But you get the point.

The Challenge:

To curate a collection of environmentally conscious pieces, epitomizing true luxury, and help Lynn look simultaneously iconic and approachable

The Baseline:

Running around town in this outfit, Lynn looks put-together and chic. But even though warm brown and camel are perfect colors for her complexion, these classic—okay, predictable—silhouettes in this monochromatic neutral palette aren't conveying her Technicolor spirit. She needs a pop.

Lynn, 50s
The Green Glamazon

CAREER: Green luxury lifestyle consultant

BASELINE WORKSTYLE: Lady in Uniform

WORKSONALITY: The Mentor

WORKPLACE: Creative, Home Office

STYLETYPE: Chic

COLORTYPE: Sun

Meeting Lynn will convince even the most skeptical style snob that green no longer equals crunchy. As an environmentally conscious developer, Lynn buys historically significant properties—and some special buildings that just appeal to her—and rehabilitates them from a green point-of-view. In addition to her renovation business, Lynn writes a column on green style; women look to her as living proof that being eco-conscious doesn't mean roughing it. Lynn is a Mentor for scores of women she doesn't even know.

Lynn was into the whole green thing before it was cool. "People were always like, she's got all these crazy things, like a wheatgrass juicer in her house!" Now, of course, a juicer is commonplace, but back then it was vanguard. "I was always afraid people would dismiss me as hippie-dippie," Lynn remembers. "But when I quit hiding my interests, the world started to open up." When a local magazine put Lynn on its cover, she talked about her passion for conservation, and the huge reader response led to her column.

Lynn believes she has been successful with her green enterprises because she has always truly believed in them; she is simply educating people about a lifestyle that comes naturally to her. "My father was a businessman who flew all around the world as an antiques dealer, but he always found the time to garden. He was into organic gardening even before people were aware of the need for conservation," she says. "He is the one who developed my sense of aesthetics and luxury—he dealt with museum-quality pieces—but he was still out in the yard at five o'clock in the morning." Her ability to truly grasp the yin and yang of a luxury lifestyle—integrating the experience of pleasure with respecting and giving back to the earth—is what makes Lynn such a special person to be around.

We wanted to help Lynn incorporate the amazing sense of ease she has in her professional life into the way she dresses. She leads a very public life, so she has to be turned out at all times. Still, it's important to her to buy environmentally responsible materials and not to be wasteful.

Lynn has a passion for Hermès bags, such as the big brown Birkin she's carrying in her baseline photo. These extremely expensive beauties might not seem environmentally conscious at first glance, but Lynn stresses it's important to think about manufacturing processes. "If you ever read about how Hermès bags are produced, they're old-world," she says. This means higher wages for artisan workers, no factory pollution, natural chemical-free materials—and, perhaps most important, an heirloom that will last for many generations. If Hermès is out of your price range—as it is for most of us—look for young brands with a commitment to handmade pieces. It's far greener to buy one or two high-ticket items that will last a lifetime than to buy into the concept of disposable fashion.

CREATIVE MEETING

Fun and Flirty

Perfect for a social event, this is a special occasion party dress. "This wouldn't have been a dress I'd pick right off the rack. At first I thought it wasn't me because of its flouncy bottom and a length shorter than what I'd typically wear. But I put it on and was pleasantly surprised!" Lynn says. We chose this dress because its seaming makes it really unusual—the sort of standout piece expected of a style icon. And although it's a very ladylike silhouette, we chose to style it a bit rock and roll with opaque tights and avant-garde heels.

FOOT NOTE: Don't be afraid to pair open-toed shoes with opaque tights. (Just make sure the toes are hole free!)

Green Power

We predict that the coming decade will be all about redefining the power suit. A power suit doesn't have to be masculine or conservative; it simply must have strong lines, natural shoulders, and an architectural feeling, conveying a sense of authority. Even in a neutral color like this one, a well-cut suit makes a strong impact. Since she is an environmentalist, people might expect Lynn to dress "earthy-crunchy," which is the opposite of the clean, polished image she wants to project as a Mentor. Appearing in public, promoting her personal brand, she should be seen in strong and simple looks in order to project sophistication, not flakiness.

116

DRESSING FOR A PRESENTATION

When planning what to wear to a presentation, imagine how your outfit would look if you were delivering the evening news on TV. If you think this sounds ridiculous, consider that an entire room of people will be focused on you—no pressure!—the same way they would on a news anchor. A news anchor dressed inappropriately might as well be spouting gibberish—wardrobe gaffes are distracting! But you remember the news a smartly dressed talking head is relaying. A tasteful, flattering ensemble will keep the attention focused on what you're saying, instead of what you're saying it in.

Here are some guidelines that will keep you looking presentable while you present:

1 Stay away from "big hair," both literal and metaphorical. What we mean is, keep all the elements of your look under the radar. Save the red dress and retro updo for the company sock hop; when you're in the spotlight you want to be sleek and subtle in every way so your performance, not your attire, can shine.

2 That said, there's no need to be boring. If you have a jacket or dress that makes you feel fantastic, wear it! The confidence it brings will surely improve your performance. Just make sure it's not too bright or tight.

3 Consider the back view. If you're writing on a white board or adjusting a projector, people will see a side of you that you rarely see yourself. Ask your mate or a colleague to tell you honestly whether the backside of a garment is too tight or see-through, or whether the lines of your underwear are visible.

4 Skip the perfume. Fragrance can fill a crowded conference room quickly, and you don't want to be known as the woman who set off the boss's allergies.

5 Keep makeup light. Nerves cause perspiration, and perspiration is the enemy of a heavily made-up face. Bring blotting papers to control shine instead of layering on the powder.

6 Wear shoes you can stand (in). When you're on your feet in front of a bunch of people you want to impress, you don't want to be shifting uncomfortably from side to side.

These Boots Were Made for Rocking

Who doesn't love a surprise? The last thing anyone would expect to see paired with a sedate, restrained little black dress like this one is a pair of crazily embellished brown boots. But to truly shine the spotlight on wearable art, hang it on a blank wall, so to speak.

118

STYLING NOTE:

Restrain yourself to one show-stopping element per outfit. People want to know where to look.

The Green Party

The key to wearing bold color is not to overaccessorize. All Lynn needs to wear with this electrifying sheath is a pair of killer heels and earrings that complement her eyes. "No matter how much time I spend preplanning my clothes before an event, I change my mind depending on my mood that day," Lynn says. We're willing to bet that she'll plan to wear this one.

From the
Desk of Darcy

Lynn's radiance is a testament to the power of a green lifestyle, proving that you are what you eat. Women aiming to avoid traditional cosmetics in favor of natural or organic ones should try mineral powder foundation—it doesn't clog pores, it offers great coverage, and many brands contain no artificial ingredients.

Ilka, 31
The Luxe Lifestyle Guru

CAREER: Business development

BASELINE WORKSTYLE: Ms. Mousy

WORKSONALITY: The Muse

WORKPLACE: Creative

STYLETYPE: Chic

COLORTYPE: Star ☆

The Challenge:
To bring a touch of femininity and joie de vivre to a serious wardrobe; to give the impression of wealth without breaking the bank

The Baseline:
Here's Ilka at her most buttoned up. This perfectly tailored suit fits her body like a glove but reveals nothing about it, from its slightly flared pant legs to its high neckline. Not bad, but a little blah. And not nearly as inspiring as a Muse needs to be.

If your job is to sell people the good life, you'd better look the part. Working in business development, a luxury lifestyle management company that handles real estate, travel, shopping, dining, and ticketing for a select group of superwealthy families, Ilka recruits new members and develops the company's profile. Because her company's 100 clients—many of them billionaires—pay $50,000 per year just to belong to the service, they expect to have contact with only the most impeccably polished representatives. This means Ilka always needs to look perfect.

Before she started in this position, Ilka worked in private wealth management at an investment bank. There, she learned the importance of dressing like a woman without revealing too much, because being taken seriously in a sea of men used to getting what they want can be a challenge. "I was asking people to let me invest their money, personally. I wanted no distraction from the conversation—I needed to look sharp but plain, bland, and conservative. Meeting with a man, I would usually wear a pantsuit: I never wanted there to be confusion about the intention of the meeting. I didn't adopt color because I didn't want to bring anything colorful to the conversation."

Transitioning from a buttoned-up financial firm to a company that concerns itself more with home and leisure than work, Ilka got the opportunity to express more personality through her clothing. Her work setting has also changed from a formal office to a much broader arena. "I do dinners all the time as well as attend a lot of charity events, gallery openings, and private parties. Of course, I spend time with our current clients, but the majority of my time is spent trying to find the right new members. It's a social job; I have to be out networking and planting seeds, so wherever I am, I'm at work. But I don't ever want to seem stuffy."

The Girl in the Gray Flannel Suit

Okay, so on the surface, it's still a conservative suit. But notice how subtle details and a little creative styling take Ilka's look from Victor to Victoria? She's showing virtually no skin here, but she still embodies femininity. The subtle fishnets, open-toed T-straps, and portfolio clutch provide a demure polish Ilka could never get from nude stockings and a run-of-the-mill work tote. Most important, the jacket's knotted neckline detail gives it a one-of-a-kind look. "In this career, I can be a bit softer because my conversation is softer. This suit is professional and conservative, but it's still feminine and fits perfectly."

FEMINIZING WITH ACCESSORIES: THERE'S NO NEED TO BE GIRLIE

In taking Ilka's tailored wardrobe from finance to fashion, we relied on the subtle punch of unusual, organic-looking accessories.

This gold cuff's irregular texture and uneven edges give it a one-of-a-kind feeling—it's as much a work of art as it is a piece of jewelry.

Even though this python clutch has a simple shape, its sleek sheen and rare material make it a standout.

Ruffled Up

See how a bottom transforms when you change what's on top? The gray pencil skirt from the preceding page goes from business to party when paired with a frilly chiffon top and wide belt. "I love how feminine this blouse is, with the ruffles—it's sheer and tastefully sexy. The back is all lace. It's the perfect way to take this suit from day to night," Ilka says.

122

STYLING MEMO:

For years, women were told to hem their work skirts just a tad above their kneecaps, but this sexy number proves that sometimes it's good to go a little longer, especially if your legs taper just beneath the knee, as Ilka's do.

Fit to Be Tied

Versatility is the name of the game with this ladylike trench/dress hybrid. Worn with boots and hoop earrings, it's great as a dress daytime look, either over a casual dress or on its own. To transition into evening, just switch boots for stilettos, and switch the hoops for diamond studs.

BEAUTY MEMO:

With a portrait collar like this one, try wearing your hair pulled up, with some height at the crown. This will elongate your neck and draw attention to your face.

LUNCH WITH A CLIENT

Under Cover

Without the trench, this dress would be "just a little bit edgy for what I do in the office—it might be bordering on too sexy from a professional perspective." But the long black trench, worn on page 123 as a dress, mutes the dress's abstract, animal-like print and disguises its close fit. Because the coat's fabric is not sporty, it is evening-appropriate.

GETTING CREATIVE

Transitioning from a formal work-place to a creative one, like Ilka has, can be intimidating. Expectations can seem unclear, and there's pressure to look cutting-edge without crossing the line into kookiness. Here are some ways to ease into a less structured environment.

Try mixing in one fun piece with your tailored favorites. A printed silk top looks great with a pinstripe suit; a showstopper necklace wakes up a shirtwaist dress.

Change your shoes. Switching out black or brown pumps for something in color provides a well-calculated punch.

Layer. Try a cashmere knit under a slinky top or dress, or a long sweater duster with trousers and a T-shirt. Besides being comfortable, layered looks convey ease and casual confidence.

Cheers!

Come evening, though, the trench comes off, and Ilka's ready for a cocktail party or a night at the opera.

STYLE COUNSEL

Advice Straight from the Hip: Katherine Cohen

Katherine Cohen, Ph.D., is CEO of IvyWise and ApplyWise, New York City admissions counseling consultancies. She advises families on how to navigate the complicated college admissions process.

When you interview a woman for a position, are there signs of grooming and dressing that you look for?

I look for manicured nails, shaved legs, and hair that is not too messy. As far as dressing, I like to see a simple chic look in clothes. However, I have hired interns who dress very avant-garde, with hair and makeup to boot. So I am pretty open. Be yourself!

Are there any red flags—wardrobe-wise—that make you worry about hiring someone?

Yes, dirty, stained, or holey clothes or open shoes like flip-flops—because it is rare to have perfect feet.

How important is it to dress for work? Is it better to be overdressed or underdressed?

I always err on the side of being overdressed. But in our office, which is not corporate, people can dress as if it were Casual Friday every day.

In terms of presenting yourself, are there things you know now that you wish you knew at the beginning of your career?

Yes! I love having basics in my closet now and did not used to purchase many of those. I used to go for detailed, unique pieces that are great for going out at night but not flexible enough for work looks.

What is the best way for a woman to assert her femininity without seeming overtly sexy?

Wear clothes that flatter the body and your natural curves. I can still look sexy in a skirt that goes below my knees and a little blazer—it is all in the cut. And always have a pair of sexy black heels in your closet; they will make even trousers look more feminine.

What are your top five dressing and grooming pet peeves at the office?

1. Be clean and showered always—smell good!

2. Manicured and pedicured is a plus.

3. Never wear clothes that are too revealing! I once had to tell an assistant to put on a bra and to stop wearing a sweater that fell off both shoulders and showed too much cleavage. That is inappropriate. No bra straps showing and not too much cleavage!

4. No flip-flops.

5. Nothing too bright, busy, or glittery. This can look clown-like or meant for nighttime. You're in an office, not a nightclub.

Natalia, Late 20s
The Shop Girl

CAREER: Manager, Jake boutique

BASELINE WORKSTYLE:
The Kooky Gal

WORKSONALITY: The Director

WORKPLACE: Creative

STYLETYPE: Bohemian Chic

COLORTYPE: Moon ☾

The Challenge:
To help a young store manager project authority and competence in a high-fashion environment on a limited budget

The Baseline:
This shapeless cheetah-print shirtdress epitomizes the Bohemian ease that has been Natalia's signature since college, and with funky accessories and natural hair and makeup, the look is still current. However, as she gains more and more responsibility at the store, Natalia wants to clean up her image. "I'm done with this dress—I'm giving it away!" she says. "I have worn it out—it just doesn't inspire me anymore. I was into it for a long time because it's playful and cool, but the shape isn't so flattering."

Natalia manages Jake, a cutting-edge high-end boutique, and has access to racks and racks of clothing any fashionista would die for. But she has exercised remarkable restraint when it comes to jumping on the latest trends: she only buys pieces that work together and has a good sense of which silhouettes flatter her shape. Still, when we met her, Natalia told us that despite her well-edited wardrobe—and extensive knowledge of fashion trends—she has a hard time wearing patterns and knowing how to accessorize. We wanted to help her create a system that would make getting dressed in the morning easy and ensure that she projects a strong sense of fashion authority. She also has to strike a delicate balance between being her store's best advertisement and not distracting from the beautiful clothes she sells.

"I fell into retail by accident," Natalia says. "I knew I wanted to be in the fashion industry, but I wasn't sure where. I've really ended up enjoying both the fashion and business parts of my job—the combination of skills required to manage a boutique really capitalizes on my strengths." Natalia believes in investing in high-quality pieces—about four per season—rather than buying lots of outfits from mass retailers. We think this is a brilliant strategy for a young woman in her late twenties who is still building her wardrobe. The only downside to her philosophy is that she grows tired of what she calls her "uniform" pieces. "I wear the same things over and over," Natalia explains. "And when the season is over, I never want to see them again."

We wanted to help Natalia choose items she'd want to look at over and over for years to come—things driven not by fashion but by fit and flattery. Although she has had Bohemian leanings since her college days, Natalia is looking to evolve her style into something more pure and chic, suited to her European heritage, and her Director Worksonality. Because she is tall and strong-shouldered, with great legs, we decided to build her look around black tights and flats, layering dresses and coats on top. "Through this process, I came to understand specifically which things really look good on me—I do well with jewel tones, strong collars, and architectural details. I think I've found my signature."

What a Jewel

This dress, another of Natalia's own, represents where she'd like to see her style going. She feels comfortable and confident in it. Since she considers herself "accessory challenged," Natalia loves that jewelry is automatically incorporated into this look via the embellished collar. "I wear this dress in the store all the time—at least twice per week. I do it with tights and boots in winter and a sheer turtleneck underneath for warmth. Key is that I can really move in it—I can wear it with flats, too. I love the bold neckline and the chic crispness of the fabric." We used Natalia's feelings about this dress to guide our other choices for her.

STYLING MEMO:

If there are stones on your clothing, don't wear them on your body, too. Less is more.

Take a Shine

Even though Natalia looks smashing in dresses, we wanted to show her that she could accomplish the same put-together ease with a skirt and top. Everyone needs great separates in their wardrobe; they provide versatility. We consider this look a bold experiment in color. This top has so much going for it—the ruffle details make it unique, but it also mixes well with everything and can be worn to work, parties, or even a night on the town. "I like bright jewel tones," Natalia says. "And I love that this top is not really fitted but also not super-balloony—it has its own shape. The skirt is really basic but great because you can wear it lots of different ways: since it's stretchy but thick, you can make it short or long, high- or low-waisted. What I really want is for my clothing to seem effortless." This leads to the confidence inherent to a Director.

BUYER MEETING

Gray Lady

Natalia is very tall and has a pretty straight figure, so she can wear loose, billowy shapes like this one. "I love the shape and the fact that it doesn't have a waist," she says. "I feel more comfortable without one." Putting on something this simple takes no effort and provides a huge payoff in a cool, artsy, I'm-a-minimalist sort of way. With tights and flats, as she's wearing it here, the look has a fall appeal. But because the style and color are seasonless, she can wear this piece bare-legged with sandals during the summer, with boots and a coat in winter, or with metallic shoes and a clutch at night. "I think the dress and the bracelet feed off each other," Natalia says.

Covering the Bases

◀ This look exudes power and would be perfect for a day working with a very important client. The coat's unique neckline has the same effect as a portrait collar: it really brings the focus to her face, almost lighting it up. Worn buttoned up with the collar popped, the coat is dressy and avant-garde. But Natalia could wear it as a layering piece during the day, with sunglasses and a scarf to make it more casual.

From the Desk of Darcy

Many natural beauties like Natalia are taught to fear color. But some people have a magical lip color that brightens their whole face, and for Natalia, it's red raspberry. This look can become a signature for her, day or night. To find your magical color, go to the makeup counter and be prepared to blot for hours. It's worth it!

The Challenge:
To inspire confidence in a mom reentering the workforce

The Baseline:
This is Alison's own go-to outfit: a gray pin-striped suit that lacks femininity and typifies the safe and stale look many women over twenty-five think of as their only option. There's nothing glaringly wrong here—this suit just makes Alison look and feel invisible. We wanted to help her show off a little, while remaining true to her Worksonality as a Nurturer.

Alison, 40s
The Comeback Kid

CAREER: Mortgage broker

BASELINE WORKSTYLE: Ms. Mousy

WORKSONALITY: The Nurturer

WORKPLACE: Public

STYLETYPE: Classic

COLORTYPE: Star ☆

Alison says she is suffering from empty-nest syndrome—but her daughter has not yet gone off to college, only kindergarten. "People say you have freedom once the kids are in school, but I miss her!" Alison says. Alison has recently begun a second career as a mortgage broker. "I chose the mortgage business because the hours are flexible—it doesn't have to be 9 to 5. We can't afford a nanny, and I don't believe in day care. I want my daughter to have the same mom time as my son did."

Like many moms reentering the workforce, Alison needs to create a professional wardrobe from the ground up. She's no stranger to fashion, but because her figure filled out a bit after she had the kids, Alison's fashion confidence had diminished. Thanks to her dance background—she is trained in ballet, jazz, and tap—her grace had not. We were excited to work with Alison because she was at a point in her life where she wanted to "relaunch herself."

Since Alison is on a tight budget right now, we shopped for outfits at discount chain stores—and found designer items at deeply discounted prices. Just because you have limited money to spend on clothing doesn't mean you shouldn't be inspired by designer looks. You can find the same styles and silhouettes at chain stores as you would at high-end boutiques. For example, one of Alison's looks was inspired by Hermès, but we picked it up at Filene's Basement.

It's a Wrap

Here's our new take on Alison's power suit. It's still gray, but the cut flatters her figure and looks more modern. The button placement—just below her bust—brings in her waist. The shorter jacket length elongates her legs. Many larger women think that they should opt for a long jacket to cover their bottom, but this actually makes the bottom seem larger.

COLOR MEMO:

Rather than accenting this gray ensemble with black, we opted for chocolate brown. Alison's tank top, wrap, pumps, and bag are all more flattering to her skin tone than black would be, and they give the look a sense of luxury.

Mixing It Up

Many people think they can't wear denim to work, but unless their office is formal, this just isn't the case. Dark denim, cut like trousers—with a wider leg and higher waist—is totally appropriate for the office. Paired with this long, cozy sweater—perfect for a Nurturer—they look comfortable and hip.

134

BARE NECESSITIES

THE FOUR LEATHER ITEMS YOU REALLY NEED

When you're on a budget, like Alison, you have to choose your investments carefully. These four items in leather and suede will work with all your career outfits.

A belt with a special buckle: To wear with trousers, skirts, belts, and jackets.

Black leather pumps: To wear with skirts, dresses, and trousers, during all four seasons.

Suede boots, in brown or black: To wear with or without tights, in cooler weather.

A roomy handbag, in brown or black: Big enough to tote work papers, not so big that it looks like a carry-on.

Hot Chocolate

Don't be afraid to shop secondhand. Many women who buy designer turn their wardrobes over every season, barely worn, and intrepid secondhand hunters can make a killing. At a designer resale store, we found a brown leather coat and matching brown knit dress, which we paired with suede boots in a slightly darker hue. This kind of tonal dressing looks rich and sophisticated.

CLOSING THE DEAL

FOOT NOTE: Notice that we paired suede—not leather—boots with the leather jacket. This keeps everything from looking too matchy-matchy. You don't want to be wearing a leather suit unless you're riding a motorcycle.

136

All Wrapped Up

Belting a wrap sweater with a thin belt instead of a thick sash is flattering and chic. This look was inspired by an Hermès ensemble we saw on the runway; it's proof that you can use styling cues from high fashion to put together a complete look at a great price. We like the mix of crinkled patent bag in black and soft suede booties in brown more than matching shoes and bag, which is too fancy a vibe for jeans.

From the
Desk of Darcy

When you have a warm, sun-kissed complexion like Alison's, the most important thing is to stay moisturized. Wear sunblock during the day and retinol at night, and your skin will keep its luster.

The Challenge:

To introduce some tradition and stability into a Whimsical wardrobe without sacrificing personal style

The Baseline:

When Susie is doing someone's makeup, she doesn't mind fading into the background. Hence, a uniform that brings to mind the coolest girl in art school—asymmetrical black separates, heavy boots, and a giant vintage schoolbag to hold all her cosmetics and tools (and her sidekick, Charlie). While there's nothing technically wrong with this look, it is a bit severe for Susie's girlish face and figure, and it's too hard-edged for someone running her own cosmetics company.

Susie, 32
The Artsy Entrepreneur

CAREER: Makeup artist and green cosmetics entrepreneur

BASELINE WORKSTYLE: Ms. Casual Friday

WORKSONALITY: The Director

WORKPLACE: Creative

STYLETYPE: Bohemian Whimsical

COLORTYPE: Earth 🌐

As a freelance makeup artist, Susie is expected to express her personality through her clothing: she can be a tortured artist in black one day and a classic, 1950s-inspired lady the next because playing with image is part of a creative person's charm. But now Susie is developing her own environmentally conscious cosmetics line, and instead of projecting "impulsive artist," she needs to convince investors and store representatives that she can be trusted to deliver a quality product.

Susie had an artist's upbringing; her father was a photographer, and her mother, a makeup artist, worked in his studio with him. After going to school for photography and graduating with a degree in art history, Susie taught for a while but didn't feel fulfilled. "I wanted to create things," she says. So she followed in her mother's footsteps and began a career in makeup artistry.

Because she's never worked anywhere with "rules," Susie's wardrobe skews heavily toward one-of-a-kind and vintage items. "I like to mix traditional things with nontraditional ones—one new piece mixed with a bunch of old vintage pieces. I like things that are unique, not mass produced. I like to walk into a room and know no one else will have what I'm wearing." This offbeat sensibility is fine when she's traveling the world on fashion shoots, but she needs to project more polish as she transitions into running her own company.

Cutting the Mustard

The first step toward freedom for black-clothing addicts is to try a monochromatic look in a dark color. Putting Susie in charcoal is one tiny change that makes a big difference. A sleek column silhouette like this one is a perfect canvas on which Susie can show off her vintage finds. We also moved her pop color—mustard—from her tote to a cardigan that's both fashionable and functional (layering is crucial for a makeup artist to work comfortably). "I do really well with wide-leg pants; I have a small waist but shorter legs, and belted high on my torso and worn with high heels, I think these pants make my legs look longer," Susie says.

COLOR MEMO:

If you're terrible at putting hues together, let a designer do the work for you. Find a print you like. Then create a look by combining items of clothing in solid colors from the print. You can find inspiration beyond the closet—try looking at vintage wallpaper for some amazing combinations.

Poster Child

This look projects a creative confidence: this is a woman who has unique ideas and is not afraid to run with them—a true Director an investor wants to bet on. This outfit is a study in color, Susie's specialty. "Makeup is about color theory, and I like to apply the same rules to my clothes as to my makeup. Once you know the color wheel, you know which shades go together. Then all you have to do is coordinate with your skin tone!"

Creating a thrown-together–put-together vibe like this one doesn't take a degree in art—just a willingness to mix different things until you discover a combination that works. The anchor of this palette barely shows at all (see that little piece of floral blouse peeking out from under the cowl-neck?), but it provides a basis for all the other shades in the outfit. The blue bag, the red skirt, and the red shoes all tie back to the flowers in the blouse. Notice how the reds of the skirt and the shoes don't match exactly? This gives the whole thing a spontaneous energy.

140

Career in Bloom

Once Susie's line is available to consumers, she'll have to spend a good part of her time meeting with magazine editors to promote it. She'll want to project friendliness, confidence, and success—and this outfit should help her score a glowing feature while showing off her Whimsical side. The pattern of this dress is reminiscent of vintage, but its cut and quality are pure designer label. The brown and taupe accessories we've chosen for her are subtle and neutral but fashion-forward, and they work back to the base colors in the print. This look shows that, even though Susie is a Director who owns her own business, she is friendly and approachable.

142

Suited for Success

An entrepreneur is her company's own best advertisement. When Susie begins to meet potential customers as her line launches in department stores, she has to present a touch of fantasy—the most fabulous version of herself. Beauty is aspirational—you're selling a lifestyle as much as a lipstick—and Susie must look like someone other women want to be. This suit will look great in press photos.

WARDROBE WISDOM:

If you love vintage but crave a more polished look, use silhouette as inspiration when shopping for new clothing. This suit combines many of the best elements of women's fashion from the 1940s—strong shoulders, a nipped-in jacket, a slim skirt—with a modern, stretch herringbone fabric and a high-fashion sensibility. Notice how we paired the look with edgy, current accoutrements—thick black tights and a rock-and-roll tote—in order to keep it looking young, modern, and not at all costumey.

From the Desk of Darcy

Because Susie was born into an artistic family, she understands her features and knows how to define them. Like many makeup artists, she focuses on skin care—thus eliminating the need for a lot of makeup. Yes, it's a teensy bit ironic.

DON'TS

1 Party clothes at the office

2 Matchy-matchy outfits

3 Chipped nail polish

4 Flip-flops

5 Visual Panty Lines (VPL)

6 Pants tucked under instead of hemmed

7 Missing buttons

8 Stains

9 Nighttime makeup

10 Big, fried hair

The Challenge:

To create a collection of truly global pieces that will fit into one fabulous suitcase and take Maye from the lecture podium to her private practice, from the park with her grandsons to the Moscow Ballet

The Baseline:

Maye often wears her favorite pair of jeans in classic blue denim with ballet flats, a white shirt, and a gray cashmere coat. It's a classic American look, but in order for it to be more polished and take her more places, we suggested she demote her beat-up denim to the weekend and wear dark denim in a sleek stovepipe fit during the workweek.

Maye, 60s
The Motivator

CAREER: Dietitian and motivational speaker

BASELINE WORKSTYLE:
Lady in Uniform / Sexy Lady

WORKSONALITY: The Mentor

WORKPLACE: Creative, Public

STYLETYPE: Chic

COLORTYPE: Moon ☾

We're not sure whether it's her South African accent, her femininity, or the fact that she looks like she stepped right out of a Hitchcock film, but Maye is the kind of woman who makes a person look forward to turning sixty. As a dietitian with a private practice in New York City, Maye sees clients who aim for optimal health—and she is the walking embodiment of her own philosophies. Along with advising people in New York, Maye travels the world to give talks, make media appearances, and promote her three books. Add to this frenetic routine seven grandchildren spread out all over the country, a mother in Canada, and a passion for adventure travel, and you've got one busy woman in the prime of her life who needs a wardrobe that can keep up with her.

We wanted to work with Maye because we feel she embodies the ideal attitude about being a mature woman—she believes she's the best version of herself at this very minute, and she wants to show it off. So often, women think they're supposed to morph into some version of their mother once their cake has too many candles to blow out. Sure, Maye takes care of her body, but, more important, she takes care of her spirit. She works hard, and she rewards herself with exciting experiences whenever she can. And she only takes one suitcase! "I just spent two weeks in the Baltic with hand luggage only," she says. "I don't care if you see me in the same outfit three times; I can't be bothered with checking!"

Creating a wardrobe suited to Maye's life might sound overwhelming, but because Maye prefers to have a few luxurious, well-curated pieces rather than a lot of stuff, it was actually rather simple. Keep in mind that the fewer items you choose to have in your wardrobe, the more special the items must be. That's why, instead of basing Maye's capsule on black or neutrals, we decided to base it on ivory. Her energy is very spiritual and light, and her blue eyes are sprinkled with white specks. And, of course, there's her glorious platinum hair and her adventurous spirit. After all, this woman jumped out of a giant birthday cake wearing a bright orange dress—at sixty. So we weren't going to put her in a black pantsuit.

Traveling Right

If you saw this woman in the airport Starbucks, wouldn't you think she was famous? At the very least, you'd want to look just like her—after all, she is a Mentor. We're all about bringing the glamour back to work travel. This look isn't overdressed for the plane, but it is put-together enough to sustain the interest of a compelling seatmate. More important, it's completely functional. The long cashmere cardigan is cozy to bundle up in on the plane, and Maye can roll it into the most luxurious neck pillow should she want to take a snooze. Black leggings won't lose their shape through hours of sitting, and flat boots travel well (and wearing them on the plane creates room in the suitcase).

MAYE'S VACATION CAPSULE

Maye recently traveled to the Baltic during the White Nights, a spectacular phenomenon requiring a spectacular wardrobe. But you know Maye's one-carry-on rule. How did she pull it off? Here, her perfect pieces for international travel:

- *Khaki raincoat:* "An indispensable piece, but by the time the trip was over, I never wanted to see it again!"

- *Lightweight sweater* for layering and keeping warm on the plane

- *Two lightweight dresses* that don't crease when packed

- *Black pants*

- *Five tops*

- *Walking shoes*

- *Flip-flops*

- *Chanel flats:* "Heels take up too much room—it's not worth it. And I think short dresses look better with flats anyway."

- *Tiny evening bag*

- *Orange Tod's handbag*

LUNCHEON

White on Target

As we mentioned before, because of her coloring and spirit, we selected Maye's capsule wardrobe in ivory rather than black, navy, or a neutral. Ivory is a fresh, youthful option for many women of a certain age—it conveys elegance and confidence and really complements platinum hair. Silhouette-wise, the turtleneck and cardigan skim her body and fit close to her shoulders, creating a long, lean look. The wide legs of her trousers cascade elegantly. Most important, they're comfortable. Maye's long pearl necklace—one of her personal favorites—was made for her by Disegno Donata. This outfit would be perfect for a luncheon or a special event because it really makes an impact.

STYLING MEMO:

Maye could switch out the cardigan for a short, fitted jacket for a more traditional look—one that would be perfect for a speaking engagement.

From the
Desk of Darcy

In all this ivory, it's important to pump up the makeup so you don't look washed out. Here, Maye's peachy lip gloss and apricot blush really help her porcelain complexion pop.

On the Go

When Maye is running around the city, she's likely to run into clients, so she always has to look fantastic. It's important that her outerwear and accessories reflect her personal style. This gray coat is cozy and luxurious and can be worn day or night. The fabulous Valentino tote, upholstered with roses, says, "I'm the kind of woman who buys herself flowers."

I WANT CANDY

FUN WITH COLORFUL ACCESSORIES

You'd be surprised how neutral a bright color can be. When we tell women to spring for shoes, a bag, or jewelry in a pop color, they often say, "But it won't go with anything!" The beauty of the right pop color is, it goes with everything. Take these red accessories we chose for Maye.

This bag suits Maye's personality—it's whimsical without being matronly. Sure, the silk roses make a major statement, but this bag is a piece of art. You'd be surprised how much wear you'll get out of a "crazy" piece you fall madly in love with.

Red shoes have been classic ever since Dorothy wore them in *The Wizard of Oz*. They look great with any neutral.

When doing major jewelry, consider colored stones. Jewel tones are super-flattering on Moons like Maye, and they bring interest to the simplest of outfits.

Lady in Red

It's possible to be va-va-voom while still covered up. This body-skimming knit dress shows off all Maye's curves. But its long sleeves and below-the-knee hemline mean it's professional enough for a nighttime work event. Red high heels, toes, and lips are a must.

From the
Desk of Darcy

Sometimes women as fair as Maye think they can't wear color, but this simply isn't true. Jewel tones will flatter translucent skin and platinum hair.

Taylor, 25
The Fashion Girl Friday

CAREER: Freelance wardrobe stylist

BASELINE WORKSTYLE:
The Kooky Gal

WORKSONALITY: The Director

WORKPLACE: Creative, Public

STYLETYPE: Bohemian, Whimsical, Classic

COLORTYPE: Earth 🌍

The Challenge:
To help Taylor transition from looking like a cool assistant to a sophisticated fashion insider

The Baseline:
"I usually wear dresses," Taylor says. "They're easier than separates because I'm 5' 1"." This look is an example of Taylor's signature eclectic style, a combination of Bohemian, Whimsical, and Classic Styletypes. A mix of neutrals is fine when your job involves supporting someone else—and sometimes receding into the background—but now that Taylor is going to take center stage as a Director, she needs to wear colors and styles that help her stand out. This dress is a bit too loose for her and looks heavy layered over black tights and a camisole. Add big, flat boots and a dowdy bag and the whole thing drags a bit—sending the opposite vibe from Taylor's bright, open energy.

Lisa Marie, a senior stylist at Visual Therapy and one of our closest friends, discovered Taylor when she was an intern working on a fashion show. "She quickly gained the respect of everyone around her," Lisa Marie says, "by displaying great energy and an upstart attitude that got her noticed." No surprise that all of a sudden she had a major job in fashion.

After a year learning the business, and getting on a first-name basis with many members of the fashion crowd, Taylor is branching out on her own as a freelance wardrobe stylist. As an assistant, her work look was comfort-driven and eclectic—she designs and sews in her spare time. But as she moves into working for herself, and developing a reputation as a tastemaker, we wanted to help Taylor step it up a bit—streamlining her style and adding authority and sophistication to her new role as a Director.

Woven Together

We wanted to show Taylor how to incorporate her handmade pieces while still keeping her look sleek and sophisticated. This jacket is very special to her: "I made this jacket a long time ago, when I used to work at a fabric store where we got end lots from super-high-end designers and manufacturers—this fabric came from Chanel. The teal, gold, and copper palette of this jacket really appealed to me—I loved it. So I made myself a coat!" This piece has a lot going on—fringed lapels and lots of texture and color—so we chose to pair it with sleek black separates and pulled-back hair in order to give the eye one place to focus.

STYLING MEMO:

You'll often hear interior designers talking about a focal point, or the element of the room your eye should be drawn to. It could be a bright wall, an oversized piece of furniture, or a work of art. This principle is based on the fact that it's more comfortable to focus your attention on one thing than to toggle back and forth between a few. You can put the same principle into practice when you dress. Pair one show-stopper piece—like Taylor's jacket—with black or neutral separates.

JEWELRY MEMO:

Taylor's signature look is layered necklaces. "They pretty much go with anything," she says. "I can wear them with a tank top, a nice piece like this jacket, a dress. I like to layer gold pendants. My boyfriend teases me and calls me Mr. T." If you feel that layering results in too much bling, you can develop your own subtle jewelry signature. Maybe you always wear diamond stud earrings or a tiny sapphire pendant. Maybe you have a ring that's a family heirloom—and even though it's a bit sparkly for daytime, it makes you happy. Wearing signature jewelry makes getting ready easy—and you're less likely to lose pieces if you're always wearing them!

Little Sparkler

People working at fashion events are often asked to wear all black. But this rhinestone-studded top is a rule-bender, allowing Taylor to blend in and stand out at the same time. These wide-legged trousers have a nice swing and create an elegant, lengthening effect—Taylor couldn't believe that, at 5'1", she could wear them.

FOOT NOTE: Hiding tall heels under long, wide-legged pants, like secret stilts, makes your legs look much, much longer.

152

Do It Like a Lady

Taylor could run a fashion show—or sit in the front row of one—in this dress, cardigan, and belt; if we saw her backstage at a major label, we'd assume she was in charge. This Classic look conveys authority and confidence; she's in control, yet still feminine. "I am so little and young-looking," Taylor says. "Sometimes I need to dress older to be taken seriously. I need to look older than I am."

AGE MEMO:

Earlier in this book, we offered a list of ways to look older than you are. Here's another: look for things that truly fit. Wearing tailored clothing takes you out of your teens and into your twenties. Switch your loose-fitting T-shirts for items that actually show the lines of your body, and you won't get carded anymore.

Royal Blue

"This would be good to throw on for a high-profile event," Taylor says. "I love cobalt. When I was little, I had a Gap mock turtleneck in cobalt, and I wore it so much it faded. I was bummed. This is like a high-fashion replacement!" This bubble-hem dress is a real knockout. It looks downtown-cool (instead of '80s-movie-extra) here, because of Taylor's low-key hair, makeup, tights, and shoes.

ACCESSORY MEMO:

When it comes to a bag for evening, we've never met a clutch we didn't like. Holding on to a clutch is so much more ladylike than throwing a strap over your shoulder, and these flat little satchels hold more than you'd think. "I usually give my boyfriend my credit card and ID when we go out—I don't even bring my phone. But when he's not with me—and I don't have a ginormous bag to carry everything in—I need a little something I can tuck under my arm and leave there all night."

Lisa Robertson, 40s

The TV Host

CAREER: TV Personality

BASELINE WORKSTYLE: Sexy Lady

WORKSONALITY: Muse

WORKPLACE: Public

STYLETYPE: Chic

COLORTYPE: Earth

The Challenge:

To help Lisa move beyond black, and show her the ease of building a wardrobe around colorful shift dresses

The Baseline:

You may be surprised to hear this, but for QVC host Lisa Robertson, "having my picture taken is like getting my teeth pulled without Novocain." Since Lisa hosts a variety of shows on the shopping channel, she needs a look that works in a variety of contexts—and conveys both her approachability and her sense of everyday glamour.

We wanted to help her put together a wardrobe that would work on air, and also off, taking things a step beyond the black separates she usually wears into someplace more colorful. "Normally when I'm putting together an on-camera look, I'm thinking about what shows I have to do—Gardening? Jewelry? Beauty?—and, usually, finding something that will work for all three is really difficult." For Lisa, we wanted to develop an easy strategy built around the idea of layering dresses, jackets, and accessories—pieces as bright and unique as she is.

"The idea of wearing color has been a real epiphany for me," Lisa says. "It's taken a long time for me to realize that black is not the only color. What real colors do for my skin tone is fantastic. I love beautiful hues: deep blues and good reds. Orange-reds and corals can look funny on camera, but that's not a problem for me—they're not my best colors anyway. Lots of prints appear to move on camera, so I stay away from them as well. And pastels are extremely affected by lighting. If the lighting is good, pastels can be beautiful—but they don't read well if it's not."

Even though Lisa has the freedom to wear whatever she wants on set, dresses are her choice because they're easy. She has a mere 60 seconds to change between shows, so there are major time constraints associated with her wardrobe. She needs pieces that can play a lot of different roles, just like she does. Since Lisa works long hours, dresses are comfortable and easy to put on, and they translate naturally from day into evening.

"In choosing styles, I go for things that show my figure, appropriately of course. Just because it is in style, doesn't mean it will look good on me," she says.

Even though this simple dress paired with a black leather jacket is perfectly chic and current, dark and monochromatic is not the wisest choice for an on-camera palette. We wanted to show Lisa that choosing brighter colors and sleeker shapes would show off her figure and really let her shine. There's nothing subdued about Lisa's ebullient personality. She should never seem like she's hiding in an outfit—onscreen or off.

Back In Black

Everyone has a little black dress. Notice how this shocking pink belt provides Lisa's hot number with an instant update—without breaking the bank. Adding a pop of color is a fun way to give a classic dress a little edge. "Even though I work in a corporate environment, I'm not considered corporate," Lisa says.

PHOTO FINISH

Here, Lisa shares her tips for looking great in front of the lens.

Most women would be amazed at the number of tips and tricks we follow to stay slim on camera. The way you stand to the camera, not what you're wearing or your actual size, is 20 pounds.

The place I learned how to stand on camera was in pageants. Of course in pageants, you're standing toward the judges, but the same rules apply. Make sure your hips are sideways while your shoulders are straight-forward. Always put your weight on your back hip; muscles that engage bunch up, while relaxed ones have a smaller look. That's why it's important to keep your front leg relaxed. If you notice in photos that you always look full in the jaw area, remember to pull your face slightly forward. Many people think you should push your chin down in order to minimize your neck. When you're twenty years old and you tilt down your chin that's a great look, but when you're forty-something, this pose exaggerates your eye shadows and softness under your jaw.

Lisa has been working with jewelry for years. Here, she shares her expertise on how to choose your baubles wisely.

The main thing to consider with jewelry is, what are you really buying it for? Will it be an investment piece, or will you wear it for a season and then be through with it? An investment needs to have quality and style. A trend piece can be cheap and cheerful as long as you don't get frustrated when it doesn't last more than a season or two.

In my mind, there are three essential jewelry pieces.
• A great watch is the watermark of a sophisticated woman. You're better off foregoing other pieces and saving up for a great timepiece that will speak for you every day.
• Every woman needs a great pair of earrings that flatter her face shape, and that she can wear with everything. I love 10mm pearl studs, simple gold buttons, or even a little hoop.
• Finally, it's important to have a go-to necklace that has a little bit more going on. But remember, any necklace that echoes down into your cleavage is not a great idea for work.

A sense of balance between your jewelry and your dress is important. If you're going to wear chandelier earrings, dress in something that's a bit more conservative. A simple sheath is always a good choice.

Pretty in Pink

Combining a fuchsia dress with a metallic, peep-toe shoe is a surefire way to brighten viewers' days—and Lisa's, too. This chain-link necklace has enough substance for daytime, but remains delicate and ladylike. Lisa states, "One thing I've noticed since working with Jesse and Joe, is the amazing difference one great bold piece of jewelry makes. I love Jesse and Joe's trick of picking one bold focal point that really draws the eye in."

156

Hip to Be Square

A wide, rectangular neckline is great for showcasing jewelry, like the crystal neck-lace Lisa wears here. We love the rich cerulean color of this dress—it's a hue that really flatters a warm Earth girl. And the closed-toe pumps make this look appropriate for day and evening—"My job requires me to go to a lot of events," Lisa says, "and I can't always wear jeans with a cool top and a statement bag—even though that's my go-to outfit."

Suited Up

Just by adding her own velvet jacket, Lisa instantly creates a power suit that's ideal for high-profile network meetings. This look really shows the versatility of using a dress as a foundation.

Film Reel Series

A pretty lady in a stylish coat creates all the anticipation of a beautifully wrapped gift. Toss a black trench over a red dress for evening, and you're all set for a grand entrance!

The difference between your trench looking sexy and dowdy is as simple as how you wear it. Tie the belt to the side—never smack dab in the middle of your torso—or you'll look like you're wearing a robe. Pop your collar for some attitude. And always choose a dark or neutral trench over a bright one for a timeless investment.

Voilà!

Few things are sexier than a red dress—especially when you keep it under wraps until the moment of your big reveal! Notice how the one we chose for Lisa is very body-conscious—it's important to create a strong silhouette when you're wearing a bright color, or your figure can get lost. Lisa's necklace really completes the look along with her femme-fatale black pumps.

You don't have to be a TV star to make a grand entrance (though in Lisa's case, it doesn't hurt).

The Career Capsule

Don't be afraid to make adjustments to your look as your career, taste, and figure go through changes. You can always retake the quizzes in this book and modify your wardrobe based on the new results. For ease in shopping, we've included a list of key items—**we call it the Career Capsule**—we believe every woman should have in her closet.

The Foolproof Career Capsule

Two or three pieces in matching fabric—some combo of a jacket, a skirt or dress, and a pair of trousers—that you can use to make a suit or wear as separates

There are many fabric options for these pieces, depending on where you live. Whichever fabric you choose, be sure it has some stretch. This will ensure a perfect fit and help the fabric keep its shape between cleanings. If you live in a place with extreme climate changes, consider buying these pieces in two fabrics (e.g., wool for winter and twill for summer).

A classic, white, button-down shirt

A versatile pantsuit or skirt suit in a solid neutral color

Three comfortable knit tops that fit your body
These could be cashmere sweaters, cotton T-shirts, camisoles, or tanks—whichever best suit your taste and lifestyle. Look for fabric blends that contain Lycra so items keep their shape.

A trench coat
This can be the traditional khaki version, but it doesn't have to be—black twill or nylon are great, too.

A pair of dark jeans in a trouser cut
A trouser cut is a more professional denim look that translates well in an office environment.

A pair of neutral flats
Depending on your Workstyle and Styletype, these can range anywhere from classic black to bejeweled metallic. Just be sure you'll be able to wear them with a variety of different things.

A pair of classic black pumps
Look for a nonexaggerated toe shape—too pointy or too round can look dated—and a feminine heel.

A pair of sturdy yet feminine boots in brown or black

A scarf or wrap in a shade (or combination of shades) from your palette

A large leather, suede, patent, or canvas work tote in a color and material that won't stain easily. You'll want it to be durable and chic.

A fun clutch to toss inside the tote and use as a handbag when running out to lunch or to an after-work event

One genius bonus of our basic work capsule is that it also provides the perfect packing list for a one-week business trip—just add undies, toiletries, and hosiery.

A Capsule-Wardrobe Resource Guide for Every Styletype

You might be wondering, shouldn't the capsule-wardrobe items differ from Styletype to Styletype? No. What will differ will be the way the pieces are interpreted through design, cut, fit, and fabric.

Take, for example, the "quintessential" black pant: For a Classic woman, it's slim and well-tailored, with a high-ish waist. For a Chic, the rise is a little lower and the leg opening a little looser. A Whimsical might want a much wider leg and pockets on the backside. Maybe a Bohemian's ideal pant has a touch of flare. And for an Avant-Garde, subtle zippers on the ankles or tuxedo stripes along the sides add that extra element that defines her style.

To find capsule pieces you love, just shop stores and designers that suit your style. Here's an easy guide.

Classic:
Agnona, Akris, Ann Taylor, Anne Klein, Brooks Brothers, Burberry, Eileen Fisher, Gap, J.Crew, Lacoste, Lilly Pulitzer, Liz Claiborne, Loro Piana, Michael Kors, Ralph Lauren, Talbots, Theory

----

Chic:
Armani, Banana Republic, Benetton, Calvin Klein, Chanel, Club Monaco, DKNY, Donna Karan, Express, Gucci, H&M, INC, Kenneth Cole, Lanvin, Laundry, The Limited, Max Mara, Narciso Rodriguez, Valentino, Zara

----

Whimsical:
Betsey Johnson, Chloe, Forever 21, French Connection, Louis Vuitton, Marc by Marc Jacobs, Marc Jacobs, Milly, Nanette Lepore, 3.1 Phillip Lim, Prada, Vera Wang

----

Bohemian:
Anthropologie, Dolce & Gabbana, Elie Tahari, Etro, H&M, Matthew Williamson, Missoni, Roberto Cavalli, Urban Outfitters

----

Avant-Garde:
Alexander McQueen, Balenciaga, Comme des Garçons, John Galliano, Jean-Paul Gaultier, Lanvin, Proenza Schouler, Topshop, Viktor & Rolf, Yohji Yamamoto, Yves Saint Laurent

Classic

Chic

Whimsical

Bohemian

Avant-Garde

CONCLUSION

We hope that the women we've introduced you to in this book have inspired you as much as they've inspired us. They are truly women of style and substance, and we learned at least as much, if not more, from them as they did from us.

The process of evolving your Workstyle and Worksonality is not something you'll do just once—it's ongoing. Keep on top of what's happening in fashion each season by browsing through department stores and looking at fashion sites online. Notice what your favorite public figures are wearing, and take inspiration from them.

Worksonality Shopping Lists

Wouldn't you love a trip to the department store to be as quick and easy as a grocery jaunt? Now it can be! On the following perforated pages you'll find handy lists to take with you as you shop for work clothes and you'll be all set for a stylish season. We've divided each Worksonality list into two categories—Cake (basics) and Frosting (stylish extras). These are not meant to be comprehensive wardrobe inventories, just suggestions of pieces that will really enrich your wardrobe.

ACKNOWLEDGMENTS

We are always grateful to our clients, incredible women of style and substance, who inspire and support us—and make our "work" feel like no such thing.

Thank you to Rebecca DiLiberto's nimble fingers for channeling our voices and ideas, and to Andy McNicol at William Morris for making this book a reality. A very special thanks to our tireless—and very stylish—editor, Jodi Warshaw, for her creativity, direction, and organization.

Eternal appreciation to our Visual Therapy team who Work It every day: Lisa Marie McComb tirelessly devoted her incredible talent and skill to this project, toiling at all hours, always looking like a '40s movie star. Sarah Davidzuk, our brilliant New York Visual Therapist, provided endless creativity, innovation, and support, with nary a glossy strand out of place. Kristi Porcelli, Rory Michaels, Asher Levine, Katy Krupp, and Jessica Sheehan contributed generously and tremendously.

Boundless gratitude to beauty guru Darcy McGrath, who provided the team with endless love, laughter, and inspiration— and left all our ladies looking fierce! Betsy Stover from 2109 Division made every day a good hair day for our models, and brilliant photographer Mary Henebry captured the essence of everyone featured in this book.

We are also grateful to Todd Okerstrom and Tina Sussman from Bergdorf Goodman, Tracy Smith from Lavande, Jake in Chicago, and Barneys New York, Chicago.

Thank you to Cynthia Holbrook from Neiman Marcus, Chicago, and Nena Ivon from Saks Fifth Avenue.

Lastly, thank you to our loving families and friends who have continued to support our dreams and endeavors through the years. You make our lives work.

snip here

THE *Nurturer*

Cake:

→ Easy-fitting suit in a neutral color
→ Linen trousers
→ Solid, pull-on dresses
→ Slim dark jeans
→ Breezy knit tunics
→ Long, cozy cardigan sweater

Frosting:

→ Lush patterned scarves and wraps that incorporate your pop color
→ Ethnic earrings
→ Bold necklaces
→ Slouchy suede boots
→ Fun flats

snip here

THE **Director**

Cake:

→ Well-tailored suit in black or navy
→ Wool trousers
→ Form-fitting shift dress
→ "Serious" blazers
→ Wide-leg trouser jeans
→ Pencil skirt
→ Body-conscious T-shirts in black and white

Frosting:

→ Status handbag
→ Bold lipstick
→ Major diamond studs (real or faux)
→ Four-inch stilettos

Notes

Notes

snip here

THE Collaborator

Cake:

- ➡ Jacket in a special fabric, such as herringbone tweed or pinstripe
- ➡ Comfortable trousers
- ➡ Easy-fitting pull-on dresses to be worn with tights
- ➡ Dark denim jeans, in both trouser and five-pocket styles
- ➡ Cashmere pull-ons in an assortment of colors
- ➡ Comfortable boots and flats

Frosting:

- ➡ Amazing leather jacket
- ➡ Fun heels
- ➡ Novel hosiery, like fishnets or ribbed tights
- ➡ Printed silk blouse
- ➡ Curve-hugging pencil skirt

snip here

THE MENTOR

Cake:

- ➡ Suit that fits like it was made for you
- ➡ Classic trench coat
- ➡ Flattering blouses
- ➡ Sleek black trousers
- ➡ Fluid knit dresses
- ➡ Wedge heels and boots

Frosting:

- ➡ Status scarves
- ➡ Luxe luggage
- ➡ Right-hand ring
- ➡ Cozy coat

Notes

Notes

THE MuSe

Cake:

➡ Flirty printed dresses
➡ Vintage-inspired skirt and pantsuits
➡ Skinny and trouser jeans
➡ Clingy knits
➡ Lush cashmere wraps
➡ Major jewelry

Frosting:

➡ High-heeled boots
➡ Funky belts
➡ Lacy underpinnings
➡ Fishnets

THE IndependeNT

Cake:

➡ Dark knit tops
➡ White button-down shirts
➡ Menswear-inspired blazers and cardigans
➡ Leggings
➡ Dark denim five-pocket jeans and trousers
➡ Lightweight trench
➡ Wrap dress

Frosting:

➡ Long, layered necklaces
➡ Signature sunglasses
➡ Zip-up ankle boots
➡ Cashmere pieces in your pop color
➡ Big, luxe tote

Notes

Notes